PLAYING THE FIELD

AUTOBIOGRAPHY OF AN ALL AMERICAN RACKETEER

By DIAMOND SPIKE

1ST EDITION COPYRIGHT 1944
8 PRINTINGS
2ND EDITION COPYRIGHT 1948

Printed in the United States of America by
NEWS PUBLISHING COMPANY
Sacramento, California

Printing Statement:

All names of Places or Persons mentioned in this publication are NOT ficticious, and reference to Persons either living or dead is NOT co-incidental.

SO-WHAT!

Distributed by

PLAYING THE FIELD

Yreka, California

CONTENTS

Dedication 7
Prelude 9
Foreword 11
Introduction 13
Son Of The Northland 17
Call Your Hand 32
The Spirit Of The Miner 33
Your Dog 34
Playing The Field 35
The Wise-Guy 49
The Biggest Little City 50
The Man That Deals The Game 51
The Dentistry Of Diamond Tooth Lill . 53
The Fiend 57
Stool-Pigeons 58
The Drunkard 59
The Ten Commandments 60
The Gambler 62
The Two-Dollar Girl 64
Woman Of Scarlet 68
The Rounder 69

Voice Of Experience 70
The Ace In The Hole 72
That Gold Miner Up Yonder 85
Take It And Live It 87
Meat On The Table Or Bust 89
Educated Fish 92
The Truth, So Help Me 94
The Crowd In The Road 96
Just Around The Corner 99
Unsung Heroines 101
Play Out The String 102
That Old Ace In The Hole 104
Confidential Advice 106
The Homecoming 108
Chips From The Diamond 134
The Summary 136
Glossary 147
Racketeers 159
Nits And Lice 162
Bees And Honey 163
Bottles And Stoppers 164
Code Of The Cannon 165
In Conclusion 168

TO TONI

The Gal who stood
    The acid test,
When the going
    Was tense and tough
Reliant and real,
    As true as steel,
A Diamond
    In the rough.

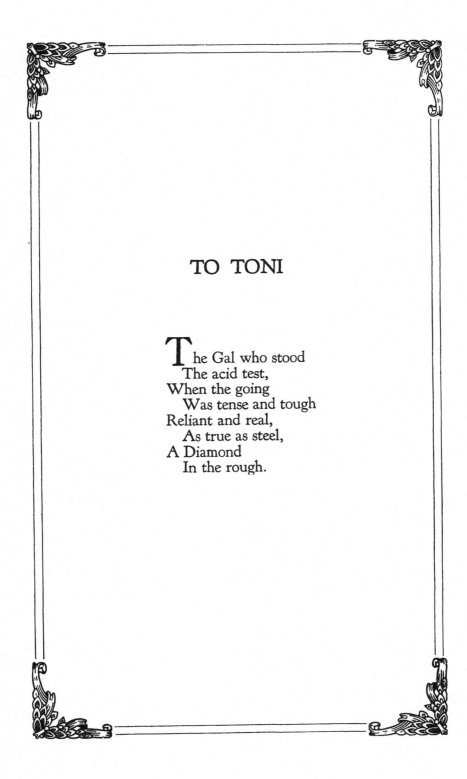

PRELUDE

You can't change
  The spots of the leopard,
The time of the tide
  Or the set of the sun;
Nor make a man content
  To lead a square life;
Who has lived
  By his wits and his gun.

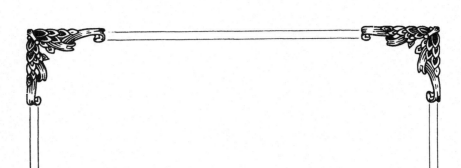

FOREWORD

"Literature consists of all the books where moral truth and human passion are touched with a certain largeness, sanity, and attraction of form."

According to the above definition, the following pages from the pen of my friend Diamond Spike can quite possibly be called literature.

The author, with disarming bluntness, has designated his opus as the "Biography of a Racketeer." His readers therefore must accept it as frankly written highlights of a life passed among the people and environment of that twilight zone which lies between the conventionally respectable stratum and the grossly criminal stratum of society — what is commonly designated as the "Sporting Class."

The verses are offered with no apologies, and apparently with little or no attempt at moralizing. Diamond Spike seems to have no desire of reforming the sporting class, among which he frankly classifies himself; and a wish for individual salvation of the classical variety also seems to be quite foreign to his thoughts. In this regard his verses are a welcome change from too, too much current writing, which must preach a sermon as a sloppy climax to a salty tale. The Diamond is openly, flagrantly, and without one hypocritical wish to be or to appear otherwise, of the earth earthy, and of the sports sporty.

And so, gentle reader, it would seem that you and I are compelled to accept the Autobiography of

Diamond Spike in the spirit in which it is offered. The "Sporting Element" is not a fantastic portion of society dreamed up and presented by some story teller. It is a distinct part, and a very real part, of the American community. He has knowingly or unknowingly given us some crassly realistic cross-sections of the half-world which merges almost imperceptibly at times with the "respectable" strata above it, and then with the murkier depths below.

P. K. CARNINE.

INTRODUCTION

The poets rant
The singers chant
Of the guilded glorious West;
Of mountains grand,
The sea, the sand,
And the desert's romantic zest.

They write full books
Of babbling brooks,
The meadows of new mown hay;
The birds and bees
The tullies and trees,
And the flowers that bloom in May.

Sweet verse they make
Of prairie and lake,
The riders of the purple sage,
The cotton, the cane
And the golden grain,
Affords them many a page.

They sing and croon
Of the Texas moon,
The beautiful Rio Grande;
The longhorn cattle—
The Alamo battle,
And the rangers who guard the land.

Biding much time
In rustic rhyme,
Of New England's rock bound coast;
The Mayflower's dock
At the Plymouth Rock,
Where the Redskins stalked as host.

Penning for days
In parable phrase,
Of the Land of the Midnight Sun;
And of sour-doughs bold
Who moiled for gold,
And thrills of the salmon run.

Though sweeter than honey
This don't get the money,
It falls short on commercial yield;
Most writers who wrote it
And poets who quote it,
Wound up in the potter's field.

Their verses and rhymes
Of western climes,
Went out with the horse-drawn hack;
That famous home
Where the buffalo roam,
Is now a tumbledown shack.

Whoinell wants to sleep
In the briney deep,
Bedfellow to a snoring sub?
Or bathe in its surf
Thick with gooey turf,
In preference to a shower or tub?

The desert's all right
If you like the sight
Of sagebrush and cactus plants;
But its romantic zeal
Loses sex appeal,
When a rattler snaps at your pants.

I don't like the looks
Of slimy brooks,
Or the stench of new mown hay;
Let the birds and bees
Live or die in the trees,
I don't care a damn either way.

The dust storms came
Ending the game,
Of the riders of the purple sage;
Now those sonzabitches
Wearing chaps for britches,
Are featured on the funny page.

The way they croon
Of that bald-headed moon,
You'd think Texas was all it adorns;
And that putrid prattle
About longhorned cattle
Who in hell wants to eat horns!

Those roguish rangers
Who shoot at strangers,
Along the banks of the Rio Grande;
Boast of records gory
Fit best in a story,
Where they end — with lily in hand.

New England's host
Of the rock bound coast,
Like the Pilgrims, have "Gone With the Wind;"
Leaving coveralls
And cod-fish balls,
When the "Grapes of Wrath" moved in.

Those bearded brutes
Who drove malamutes,
In the Land of the Midnight Sun;
Have either turned thief
Or gone on relief,
I should know — because I was one.

Now for merit and might
A writer must write
On the subject he holds most dear;
So I picked for my taw
That headache to John-law,
The All-American Racketeer.

I'm not a Shelley,
A Burns or a Kelly,
Nor an exploiter of exotic joke;
Don't want my name
In the Hall of Fame,
All I want is — "Pape in the Poke."

Took nerve to do it
The FBI drove me to it
Since they placed the rackets on strike;
So — for commercial yield
I give you "*Playing the Field*"
THE AUTOBIOGRAPHY of Diamond Spike.

SON OF THE NORTHLAND

Born
In the heart of the Arctics,
Where the North Lights
Flare out in bars;
And blasts of the wind
Play weird music,
While wolves
Howl their song to the stars.

First son
Of "Bad Bob," the boss facteur—
That he-man
Of Hudson Bay fame;
Who in camp
Was meek as a kitten,
But on trail
Lived bang up to his name.

My mother—
No sweeter was ever;
An angel,
God rest her soul;
On her shoulders
I leaned for my learning,
There were no schools
Round the pole.

My vocation—
Just one route to follow
In that unharnessed
Land of the sun;
Where man
Banks his bid for existence
On strength
And skill with a gun.

Was Taught
Reading and Writing,
From books
We got through the mail;
Learned the law of the north
From trappers,
Who spent their whole lives
On the trail.

"Bad Bob" — of course,
Was the idol
Of my youth's
First fancies and dreams;
As rough life
Hardened my sinews,
Other heroes appeared
On the scenes.

For one
I held great admiration,
A French Canuck,
"Smiler" La Bian
The type you meet
One in a million—
A smiling face,
With the heart of a lion.

A superman,
If God ever made one,
With qualities
Of unmeasureable worth;
Staunch, true
To mankind and nature,
In my eyes,
The salt of the earth.

Ever willing
To shoulder your burden;
A friend in need,
First to the bat;
Right or wrong
He'd stick to the finish,
And would fight—
At the drop of the hat.

As a musher
He'd scarcely an equal,
As camp jester
Drew happy applause;
His virtues
"Spreading the sunshine";
His sins,
Old wine and young squaws.

With him I would hold
Secret council,
Concerning the ways
Of the trails,
Ambitious to be a facteur
Like Father—
Big, strong,
And tougher than nails.

He taught me
To mush with a dog team;
Lash a sled
So the pack wouldn't slip;
Cook, eat and sleep
In a snowdrift,
Fight, swear,
And shoot from the hip.

"These teachings"
He said, "are essential
To build a man
Fit for the trail;
You'll never learn to be
Like your father
From those books
You get through the mail."

On the eve
Of my sixteenth birthday
They hauled "Bad Bob" in,
Lashed on a sled;
In a hand-to-hand fight
With a grizzly
He'd been torn
From his feet to his head.

Without sanction
I harnessed a dog team;
'Fore the men of the camp
Could surmise
Was burning the trail
Toward the boundary,
For a doctor
And needed supplies.

Soon discouraged
Well-meaning pursuers
With bluffs
From my forty-four gun—
They knew my chance
Of following that trail
Was less
Than a thousand to one.

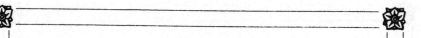

Mushing into the teeth
Of a blizzard,
Closing in
With the grip of a vise;
Blotting out
All marks of direction,
A sheet of blinding snow
And driving ice.

The Duty Law,
"The Smiler" had explained it,
Was applied,
Same as hauling the mail;
If you start
On a mission of mercy,
Fight through—
Never backtrack the trail.

On and on,
With no regard for self or huskies,
Fighting blindly
Through that haze of howling hue;
Trusting fate
To guide my true direction,
And God
Give me strength to carry thru.

With little care
For dangers encountered,
With less care
For hardships endured;
Concerned only food
For the dogs suffice,
Till a break in the storm
Was assured.

Miles and miles,
We wandered, weaved and wallowed,
Like a helpless ship
Upon the raging main;
Hours and hours
Of hazards unrelenting,
Days and nights
Of misery, hunger, pain.

True to type
Of northland blizzards,
That come and go
Without warning; their ways;
A sudden change of wind
A welcome chinook,
And the sun
Shot its warmth through the haze,

With the calm
I could sight our destination,
Fate played her part,
And played it mighty well;
I breathed a prayer
Of thankfulness to heaven,
I'd won the race
Against that howling hell.

The dogs were spent,
But quickly sensed the victory,
Howled out their gratitude
In curdling wail;
Except their leader,
On the sled bound and bleeding,
With his forefeet cut to shreds
From breaking trail.

The mush back home
A pleasure canter,
With fresh huskies
Friends of Father had supplied;
Though a heavy doctor
Crouched between the handles,
I seldom stopped to eat,
Rest, or ride.

I banked my sled
In front of Father's cabin,
The camp sent up
A deafening shout of joy;
Mother's face beamed smiles
Of admiration,
As she greeted me and cried,
"God bless my boy!"

This earned for me
The true rights of the musher,
I had proved my metal
On the trail;
Soon was
In the parka of a packer,
Hauling fur packs,
Supplies and companv mail.

In three years,
On advice of doctors,
"Bad Bob" was persuaded
To retire;
Though he trail ruled
With sterness of a monarch,
He left a record
Real Northmen still admire.

"Fair dealing"
His motto and watchword,
"Live and let live"
His practice and belief;
A helping hand
To any man on the level,
Plain poison
To a liar or thief.

The day
He was leaving the snowland,
I was lashing the packs
On his sled;
He unbuckled
His hand-knife and six-gun,
Strapped them
Tight 'round my waist as he said:

"I leave these,
Your protector and guardian,
With my serious advice
To you, son;
The surest way in this land
To get justice,
Is by the bark
Of your forty-four gun.

"I regret fate has willed
My departure,
Though I am proud
To surrender command,
With my son;
To fight on as facteur,
And rule the trails
Of this merciless land.

"Score true to the mark
Of your training,
Be just, fair
And quick on the draw;
Use sound judgment,
If caught in close quarters,
Make the six-gun
Nine points of your law."

Then he shouted,
"Good-bye, all, God bless you;"
Nosed the gee-pole
Toward the southwest trail;
Cracked his lash
Yelled "mush" to the huskies,
Gliding away
Like the gust of a gale.

In full charge of the trails
Of that wasteland,
Where the colt-gun
Is the unwritten law:
To follow the footsteps
Of my father,
Dealing square,
But damn quick on the draw.

But the gold lure
Kept beckoning and beckoning,
Till my grip on the fur trails
Failed to hold;
Soundly seized
With a drawing desire,
To join that mad scramble
For gold.

The old "Smiler"
Was dead anxious to enter
The conquest
Of shovels and picks;
We hit the trail
For the Endicott Mountains,
To make or break
On the gold-bearing creeks.

Fighting weeks
To reach the icy uplands,
Breaking trail
Through a sea of crusted snow,
Pitching camp
Without protection or shelter,
With weather
Sixty-five degrees below.

It took guts
To face that hell of hardship,
And strength
Of tempered steel and iron mail;
But there's something
In the glamour of the gold-rush,
That drives you on
Till you drop dead on the trail.

To guide the sleds
And scale those lofty summits,
That loomed up
Like huge beacons in a fog;
Took technique
Only known to seasoned mushers,
And superhuman strength
Of man and dog.

The last few days, to me,
Were a nightmare —
Snow-blind, half mad
From bitter cold;
I visioned the dogs,
Were prancing horses,
And sleds were wagons
Filled with shining gold.

Gained the pass
Started on the downward
The weather cleared
With scarcely any snow;
We rallied at the sight
Of our objective,
Winding creeks
In the valley just below.

We arrived with happy hearts
And high ambitions,
Though the hardships
Wrot us weak as men of tin;
We made a vow
As we staked our locations,
We'd stick right to the creek
Until we win.

The summer sun
Soon put me back to normal,
But the Smiler seemed to lose
In strength and weight;
Though he'd only smile and joke
When I advised him
We seek a doctor's aid
Before too late.

As summer
Drifted into chilly autumn
He had wasted
To the thinness of a knife;
It was plain to see
That trip across the mountains
Had stamped its brand
Upon The Smiler's life.

When winter hit
He rarely left the cabin,
One day I found him
Writhing on the bed;
I touched his flesh,
It fairly burned with fever,
That cursed plague
All northmen live to dread.

His weakened state
Made him an easy victim,
Within a week
The Supreme Dealer cashed him in;
As he died, he smiled and said:
"Don't weaken, partner;
Stick right to the creek
Until you win."

You could never half conceive
The grief and sorrow
I experienced
That cold December day;
As I laid my pal to rest
Beneath the hillside;
And knelt beside his grave
As I did pray.

"Our Father,
Who art in heaven,
The Old Smiler
Has answered your call;
Thy will be done,
But you've robbed me
Of my partner, my friend,
My all.

"You must have been wanting
A helper,
Sized up all men
For their worth;
Settled your choice
On the Smiler,
The best qualified
Man on earth.

"Now, dear God,
When you need a vacation,
From your post
As Facteur on high;
You can leave him in charge
Without worry,
You'll find him
Square as a die.

"Charge my account
With his sinnings,
Make his record
Clean as new snow;
Let him mush the golden trails
Of heaven,
I'll mush the Hell trails,
Here below."

My thoughts I leave
To your imagination,
As I staggered blindly towards
That empty shack;
From the place I'd carried
My old partner
To the end of his earthly trail,
Upon my back.

Completely overcome
With grief and sadness,
I hit my bunk
And fainted dead away;
With frozen hands and feet
I was awakened
By the huskies,
Holding hungry wolves at bay.

Time will never blot the scene
From my memory,
Of those huskies,
Like soldiers, grim and brave;
Showing love and devotion
To the Smiler,
By standing constant vigil
O'er his grave.

Through lonely nights
And dreary days that followed,
All alone, trail-blocked in
By drifting snows;
Like a ship-wrecked sailor
On a barren island—
How I kept from going mad,
God only knows.

Signs of Spring
Came like a gift from heaven;
The first warm day
I sharpened up my pick;
Could 'most forget the horrors
Of that winter,
As I worked from morn till night
Along the creek.

All summer long
I scrambled in that mire,
Ere I hit
A streak of heavy yellow pay;
The news spread out
And brought a ready buyer,
I sold out
Claims and all without delay.

I packed my sled,
Hit the trail for Dawson,
For me the land of gold
Had lost its lure;
Homesick for a sight
Of Dad and Mother,
A trip out to the States,
The only cure.

Caught the boat
And started down the river,
My reward of satisfaction
Just begin;
I'd kept the vow
Made my dying partner,
Stick right to the creek
Until you win.

CALL YOUR HAND

If you like a person—
Show it,
Speak right up
Let him know it.
If you think he rates your praises,
Call your hand.
Don't withhold
Your admiration,
Till he's reached
Life's destination
And they shuffle him
Beneath six feet of sand.
Better than
Post-mortem giving,
Is to help him
While he's living;
Let him hear the words of friendship
You have said.
Don't put off
Till dirge is chanted,
And "X" marks the spot
He's planted,
He cannot smell the flowers
When he's dead.

THE SPIRIT OF THE MINER

Welcome to my cabin,
  STRANGER!
Hope you find things
  Clean and good;
Feel right at home,
  And when you're leaving
Kindly fill the box
  With wood.

YOUR DOG

Just the same,
Through days of sunshine
Just the same,
Through nights of fog;
Ever with . . . .
Always for you . . . .
Your most faithful friend —
Your DOG.

PLAYING THE FIELD

A sapling
From the snarling snowlands,
Grown wild
'Neath the shade of the Pole;
Where bacon and beans
Is the high card,
Sourdough bread
Your ace in the hole.

Six foot three
Of health and high spirits,
Without a thought
Of the future's yield;
Though mother
Had hopefully visioned
My calling be
The pastoral field.

Bad Bob
Bellowed disapproval,
With allusions
"Wild oats must be sown;
There's time
To save souls of others,
When damn sure
You can save your own."

Undissuaded,
I put forth an effort,
Undaunted,
Without bauble or bluff;
Till a modern Eve
Tossed me an apple,
Like Old Adam,
One bite was enough.

After a trip
Through the Garden of Eden,
I was a bust
From the tap of the gong;
Sidetracked
From the path of righteousness
Onto the trail
Of wine, woman and song.

Started parting my hair
In the middle,
Button shoes
Replaced my high boots;
A quick change
From the raiment of the righteous,
To silk-shirts
And box back suits.

Dealt off dough
Like a sailor on shore-leave,
Rode the rough end
Of many a joke;
Took the chides on the chin,
Like a champion,
There was plenty
Of pape in my poke.

Past performances
Prompts a proven proverb,
Safe and sure
As the set of the sun;
Although the sucker
Must finance the fiddler,
He dips his duke
Into most of the fun.

A season's sailing
On the sea of society,
Polished my primitive
Pinfeathers down,
Docked me
In the world's oldest racket,
Commonly called:
"The Man About Town."

My first light-o-love
Was a red-head,
An outlaw fluzzy
Named Fay,
Branded a bad bet
By "the talent,"
To my views
The best bet of the day.

Her hair flared
The flames of the sunset;
Her eyes,
The deep blue of the lakes;
A form,
Like the statue of Venus,
Plus everything else
That it takes.

"A sour score"
The wise Willies warbled,
Tho' sweet to me
As the flowers in May;
To hit the kip
The "Akta" on the dresser,
Amid the aroma
Of Cashmere Bouquet.

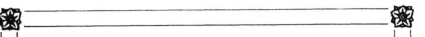

Ere a month
Hurled into history,
I detected a decline
In the take;
A scarcity
Of rattlers' hisses,
Lovingly lavished
When first on the make.

Thus entered
The green-eyed monster,
With other demons
In on the play;
Though I devolved
In tireless combatment,
My light-o-love
Kept drifting away.

One evening
While casing her travels,
Saw her hotfoot
To a pipe-puffer's room;
When she bounced out
Banged to a million,
There and then
I lowered the boom.

The next night
Entering the shovel,
Was knocked for a row
When I found
She had powdered,
Bag and baggage,
Leaving a message:
"I'll see you around."

Thus ended
My first road to romance;
The thought of it
Long made me scorch.
She had joined out
A hop-head from Texas,
Boy! . . . . Oh, Boy! . . .
Did I carry that torch! . . .

I sour-graped a boast
To the barkeep
While drowning my sorrows
In Scotch:
"If I tumble
For another damn hop-head,
I'll guarantee
To give you my watch."

"Fair enough, Baby Shoes,
That's a wager."
Then he tossed
A fat fly in my stew:
"You're not figured
A first-class flounder
Till you blow one
To a Chino or Blue."

For a time it was
Hit it and take it,
In all games
Concerning the heart,
Felt just the same
At the blow-off
As I did
When making the start.

The love bug
Again nipped me in Dawson,
It seemed
I was cold-decked by fate;
I fell
Like a carload of concrete,
For the "Toast of the Klondyke,"
Named Kate.

To tip you off
To her trimmings is useless,
Northern history
Has handed that down;
Simply a flower
In any man's garden,
A shining jewel
In any man's crown.

At the time,
She was wining and dining
With an undersized Greek
They called Pan;
I high-pitched
I'd tear down his playhouse,
If it took the last
Cake in my can.

The speed of the race
Had him rustling
All the dough he could
Beg, borrow and steal,
To bounce
For her restaurant markers,
She sopped up
Six eggs at a meal.

Now, hen fruit
In that neck of the nation,
Was considered
A luxurious treat;
You laid out
Five kopeks a copy
For each and every egg
You would eat.

A wise idea appeared
Out of nowhere,
'Twas like Old Aladdin
Rubbing his lamp; —
I'll corner the damn market
On hen fruit,
And starve her
Into my camp.

Zooming forth
With the zest of a zephyr,
Catch-as-catch-can
No holds barred;
Buying everything
From dough gods to door knobs,
By weight or size,
Dozen or yard.

Eggs — fresh, frozen
And rotten;
Eggs — by basket,
Barrel and sack;
To this day
The mention of henfruit,
Causes a pain
At the stem end of my back.

When success
Seemed sure and certain,
With most of the fruit
In my fold,
The tip leaked,
Up jumped the market;
You would think
They were plated with gold.

What caused the turn
In the market
Was as plain as
The snozz on your face;
The "Pappas" got hip
To my racket,
And was giving me
A hell of a race.

But . . . . faint heart
Ne'er cold-decked a draw game;
I bucked the tiger
Straight through the deal,
From the "top of the box"
To the "cat hop,"
Never missing
A turn of the wheel.

When fortune smiled
On my efforts,
I was clean
As the trunk of a tramp;
But gloried in the
Satisfaction,
I owned
Every damn egg in the camp.

Throwing scrambled egg parties
At random,
Soon had the race
Packed in the bag;
Plowed the deep
On the high weeping willow,
While old Pantages
Was packing the flag.

This blissful romance
Based on hen berries,
Took a Houdini
The following week,
She suddenly sickened
Of omelets
And returned to that
Half-a-pint Greek.

Revengeful o'er the ruin
Of this romance,
I placed those eggs
In a lug,
Tossed them
At the "Toast of the Klondyke,"
They tossed me
Slap bang in the jug.

"Fifty bucks," said the judge,
"Do you have it?"
"Yes . . . in small change,"
I sarcastically spoke.
"And . . . . sixty days work
On the wood pile;
Do you have change
For that in your poke?"

Venting my vengeance
On that wood pile,
A new angle
To my thoughts had appealed,—
Not to put all my eggs
In one basket,
Make a switch in my play
To the field.

Science says
There is safety in numbers;
From then on
I played for them all;
Bleached blondes, brunettes,
And what have you?
Placing plenty of stuff
On the ball.

Conceiving the idea
Of the chain store,
The origination of this
I can boast;
Established a chain stable
Of starlings,
That had the Safeway
Tied to a post.

Building up a
"Take by mail" business,
With home offices
At Kearney and Pine;
My territory
Extending
From the North Pole
To the Mexican line.

Made calls
Like a traveling salesman,
Lugged two keesters
Specially made,
Full of "thesies and thosies"
And silken kimonas,
They used
In the tricks of the trade.

For a sideline,
I sailed in for gambling,
As a diversion
While making my stops;
Learned to run up a duke,
Snare a second,
Switch a cold-deck,
Toss in the tops.

This proved to be
Eggs in my coffee,
It paid off
In profit and fun;
Heretofore,
My gambling ventures
Were confined to my skill
With a gun.

Ever eager to high roll
A crap game,
Laying the odds
They didn't or did,
In one game
I won a twist named Lilly
From a gambler
Tagged "The Swingingdoor Kid."

This contest will be
Meshed in my memory
Till St. Peter makes out
My last bill;
The prize bet
I won in that crap game
Was the world famous
"Diamond Tooth Lill."

Compared to my
Numerous entries,
She was miles
The pick of the lot,
I fell for her,
Hook, line and sinker,
And I do'ed her
Right on the spot.

Dead willing
To work double harness,
Took her place
At the head of the class,
With full authority
To hire and fire,
And make them all
Step on the gas.

We pulled together
Like a team of trained huskies,
Each seriously doing
His stuff;
Find 'em, play 'em, make 'em,
Take 'em,
Leave 'em,
When the going got rough.

Playing the con
Was pea on her paddle,
Patience to angle for days
With a pest,
Would stick
Till the very last button
Was clipped
From the cloth of his vest.

She led many a lamb
Up to slaughter,
Truly thrilled
At results of her steers;
The moaning and groaning
Of a sucker
Was sweet music
To her casehardened ears.

Years we worked
Shoulder to shoulder,
In the vocation of
Grabbing the glue,
Got more kick
From the course of the conflict,
Than we did from
Padding our shoe.

When Uncle Sam
Sent out the signal
For he-men to
Hamper the Hun,
I relinquished my role
In the rackets
To do my bit
At the butt of a gun.

The big scramble
Caused the bust-up with Lillie,
'Twas like the verse
Of that popular song:
"You went away
Too far a distance,
And stayed away
A little too long."

Now I am
Callous and hardened
Against torching o'er
The loss of a dame,
Dismiss it
As only a trifle,
Like making a bad call
In a game.

I did the world war
In a cake walk,
Finished the race
Well under wraps,
With medals galore,
And a bankroll,
I won
In the Battle of Craps.

As soon as
They slipped me a discharge,
And the wound in my leg
Was all healed,
I rejoined
The army of rackets,
To take my best shot
PLAYING THE FIELD.

THE WISE-GUY

Came depression,
  Unexpected;
Wise-guy's bank-roll,
  Unprotected;
Loudly wails
  "Unnatural break;"
Sorrowfully senses
  Diminishing take;
Recovery attempts
  Reversed by fate;
To Soaksville goes
  The family plate.

While the pitied sucker
  On yonder farm,
Unaffected
  By depression's harm,
Markets milk
  From contented cows,
Ditto pork
  From fattened sows;
Un-harrassed
  By fate's unsteady hand,
Cadillacs to the bank
  With another grand.

Reminiscence
  Of that age-old yarn: —
"The Wise-Guy sleeps
  In the Sucker's barn."

THE BIGGEST LITTLE CITY

Gorgeous, glittering,
   Undismayed;
Unabashed
   And unafraid;
Glamour and gaiety
   Rule supreme;
Gallantry, chivalry,
   Tact extreme;
Compassionate,
   In friendships' bind,
Benevolent
   To all mankind.
Fair in tactics,
   Square in trade,
Where a promise given
   Is a debt that's paid,
And man is judged,
   By act and deed,
Not by riches,
   Race or creed;
Good-fellowship,
   In harmonious swing,
Reno, my Reno,
   Of thee, I sing!

THE MAN THAT DEALS THE GAME

Sport records feature the fighter,
  Drivers of boat and car,
Ballplayers, wrestlers, golfers,
  And the man behind the bar;
There's one man seldom mentioned,
  In sportdom's hall of fame,
The man behind the layout
  That deals the gambling game.

Did you ever note the rhythm,
  And the finesse as he deals,
The bounding dice, the glist'ning cards,
  The gaudy, whiring wheels?
Did you ever pause to figure,
  The fitness that's required,
Of the man behind the layout,
  Before he's placed or hired?

He must have a neat appearance,
  Prove a record free from taint,
Be tactful as a jurist,
  Be patient as a saint;
Be ever gentle mannered,
  With the public he must vie,
A good judge of human nature,
  Quick of hand and sharp of eye.

Be sympathetic when you're losing,
Be exultant when you win,
Hold himself in strict accordance,
With whatever mood you're in;
Bear the brunt of misconception,
If the peace he can induce,
Oft the object of inference,
And the target for abuse.

But he smiles and sings his rhythm,
Of all reproach he is beyond,
Standing wholly on his honor,
With his word, a sacred bond;
A faithful servant to the public,
Win or lose he's just the same,
A credit to the world of sportdom,
Is the man that deals the game.

THE DENTISTRY OF DIAMOND TOOTH LILL

Gather 'round
   I'll slip you the lowdown,
Although
   It dampens my ardor to spill;
What prompted
   The placement of brilliants,
In the kisser
   Of Diamond-tooth Lill.

Just at the age
   When ego
And confidence
   Runs highest tide;
To excell
   In each undertaking
My earthly
   Ambition and pride.

Especially proud
   Of my six-gun talent,
Would oft bet
   All the gilt in my kick;
Snuffing a candle
   At twenty-five paces,
Without leaving
   A mark on the stick.

My heartiest booster,
Was Lilly,
At the time
My number one Muff;
Ever willing
To act as accomplice,
While I put on
My William Tell stuff.

One large night
In a dancehall at Fairbanks,
I wagered
Five hundred bucks gold
I'd shoot
And dust off the ashes
From the cigarette
Lill had just rolled.

Thus exciting
A wave of wagering
That spread
To other spots on the line;
They were betting from
Dollars to doughnuts,
From dog-teams
To bottles of wine.

The camp buzzed
With excitement,
Fast action
On every hand;
The Elmer dared
Double the wager,
I called him
And raised him a grand.

The bartender
   Paced off the distance,
A goodly crowd
   Gathered 'round in a ring;
The band played
   Hearts and Flowers,
With a drunken twist,
   Trying to sing.

Lill stuck the pill
   'Twixt her choppers,
My gat spat
   With deafening roar;
When the smoke cleared
   To enable my vision,
There was Lill
   Flattened out on the floor.

There was a mad rush
   For the exits,
The bartender
   Tossed in the towel;
The landlady
   Sent a call for a croaker,
The drunken twist
   Started to howl.

It may have been
   What I'd been eating,
Must give
   Something or other the beef;
My shot
   Had gone an inch to leeward,
And knocked out
   Four of Lill's teeth.

Imagine
  My pride, at that moment,
It had sunk
  To the height of a louse;
I paid off my bets
  Like a major,
And sailed for drinks
  For the house.

In a gesture
  Of consolation,
I said: "Lillie,
  We'll hit for the south,
I'll replace those pickets
  With diamonds,—
I'll stick a jewelry store
  Right in your mouth."

The next spring,
  She showed up at Fairbanks,
Looking trim
  As the bark of a birch;
Her hair
  Bleached the color of cotton,
Her kisser
  Lit up like a church.

In case
  You have doubts of this story,
And you think
  I'm a chump with a gun;
Pace the distance
  Light your own candle,
Get something up, —
  I'm laying two to your one.

THE FIEND

Numbed
  By nauseous nectars;
Dumbed
  By deadening drug;
Snubbed
  By society's solidity;
Shunned
  By layman and thug.

Raving
  With fallible fancies;
Craving
  With delirious desire;
Clothed
  In the cloak of contagion;
Loathed, —
  A licentious liar.

Monster
  Of malice and misery;
Sponsor
  Of duress and dread;
Molecule
  Of manhood's metal;
A damsight better off
  . . . . DEAD.

STOOL-PIGEONS

Degenerate gender,
   Gruesome as gore;
Stenching, stagnant,
   Rotten to the core;
Un-meritorious manure,
   Mendaciousness en masse;
Scurrilous scorpions,
   Snakes in the grass;
Dishonorable derelicts,
   Deplorable in deeds;
Contemptible, cowardly,
   A curse to all creeds;
Villainous vagrants,
   Valueless in worth;
Snoopers, stool-pigeons —
   SCUM OF THE EARTH.

THE DRUNKARD

Stupified
   With stimulants;
Steeped
   In stenching rum;
A doltard
   Of debauchery;
Destined —
   To be a BUM.

THE TEN COMMANDMENTS

Love thy neighbor as thyself,
  Whether Gentile, Jap or Jew;
Except in a game of poker,
  Take him ere he takes you.

♦ ♦ ♦

As ye sow, so shall ye reap,
  This life is what we make it;
Therefore, he who puts it out,
  Some day will have to take it.

♦ ♦ ♦

Knock a knocker, boost a booster,
  Play the game of give and take;
Never try to cheat a cheater,
  Or give a chump an even break.

♦ ♦ ♦

Play 'em, if they're simple;
  Make 'em, if they're tart;
Take 'em, if they're easy;
  Leave 'em, if they're smart!

♦ ♦ ♦

When things get tough, get tougher;
  Keep your runner in the rut;
Stick right to your peanut-stand,
  If you never sell a nut.

♦ ♦ ♦

Keep yourself in circulation,
  Show the world you're still alive;
The bee that gets the honey,
  Doesn't hang around the hive.

Have your share of earthly pleasures,
Get your fill of wine, woman and song;
Follow the lines of least resistance,
You won't be here for long.

♦ ♦ ♦

Don't waste energy in bragging,
Let results, your deeds reveal;
The steam that blows the whistle
Will never turn the wheel.

♦ ♦ ♦

If at first you don't succeed,
And are thrown for a loss or fall;
Substitute strength with strategy,
Stick more stuff on the ball.

♦ ♦ ♦

If you would make speed up the ladder
To the success you desire to win,
Do a little less broadcasting,
And much more listening in.

THE GAMBLER

He lives in the circle
   Of nobody cares;
Maybe a bit brazen,
   He's shorn;
The subject of whispers,
   The object of stares,
Of pity, perhaps,
   And of scorn.

His past is a subject
   He will seldom recall;
The future
   Is only a joke;
Lives as he gambles,
   On the "drop of the ball";
His life trussed
   To an uncertain yoke.

Recognized by the gang,
   A few short years;
Fast living
   Slows up his pace;
Cashes in his chips . . . .
   Fades away . . . disappears . .
A new player
   Takes his place.

His going invokes
   Neither whimper nor whim,
The game goes on
   Just the same;
He asks no man
   To feel sorry for him,
He's gone —
   It's all in the game.

THE TWO-DOLLAR GIRL

Hello, there! . . . handsome!
  How's about it;
No — I don't mean
  Dine or dance;
Yes — two dollars
  Is the stipend;
Come on — Big Boy!
  Take a chance.

Now — Don't get
  Quite so familiar,
Discard your hand
  Before the deal;
Table stakes are
  Quite in order,
Coin of the realm
  You must reveal.

I'm out strictly
  For the silver,
A lover's comforts
  To provide;
Take your choice,
  Treat, trade or travel,
Let your conscience
  Be your guide.

So! . . . You think
I'm cute and classy,
You are lonesome, —
That's a shame;
And you'd take me
Off the pavement,
If just with you
I'd play the game.

Then we'd find
A cozy cottage,
In some secluded,
Quiet nook;
With an arbor
And a garden,
Like the pictures
In the book;

Where I could have
A dog and kittens,
Perhaps,
A child or two;
I'd never
Have a worry,
No — just leave it
All to you.

Say! . . . I'm wise
To the antique angles
All you Squarejohns
Try to pull,
I deal only
Cash-and-carry,
With transactions
Paid in full.

. . . . Can the soft stuff,
Let's get going;
You'll feel different
When you're through;
That's why I'm in
This rotten racket,—
Believing men
The type of you.

Trusting men
Was once my weakness,
Fell for every word
They'd say;
All about that
Home and fireside
We were sure to have
Some day.

Just to have them
Chill and vanish,
When they'd satisfied
Their greed;
Till I wound up
In the gutter,
With a baby's mouth
To feed.

I took the only
Route left open,
I'm content
To face my doom;
Is it worse
To sin for money
Than to sin
For board and room?

Thank you kindly
   For the offer,
I'm no longer
   In that whirl;
Satisfied
   To pound the pavement,
And be a plain
   Two dollar girl.

I've a man
   I'm plenty hot for,
As for you
   I'm cold as ice;
So — get it out
   And bounce it, sucker!
Yes — two dollars
   Is the price.

WOMAN OF SCARLET

Why scoff
At result of misfortune,
Who are we
To judge her line?
Remember — ere her trust
In some rat of a man,
She was pure
As your sister or mine.

THE ROUNDER

Kindly greet
  The Rounder.
He is human,
  Nothing less.
Let a kind word,
  Softly spoken,
Soothe a tired heart
  To rest.

Though he's hardened
  By the rackets,
And his face
  Looks cold as stone,
The heart
  Within his bosom
Beats as kindly
  As your own.

VOICE OF EXPERIENCE

I've learned from dear experience,
  I'll pass along the tip—
The longest span of life
  Is from the holster to the hip.

♦ ♦ ♦

If you doublecross a Chinaman,
  Or cheat him of his stack,
He'll never beef, or holler bull,
  He'll call and raise you back.

♦ ♦ ♦

(What's the cause, I've often wondered,
  You'll agree it's not a joke;
We always get the hungriest
  The minute we go broke.)

♦ ♦ ♦

(You can't drive a nail or motor,
  Cook a meal or pack a trunk;
There's nothing in this world you can
  Accomplish, when you're drunk.)

♦ ♦ ♦

Whether north, east, south or west,
  In the country, or city's hub,
The only way you'll ever get justice
  Is with a gun or a piss-elm club.

♦ ♦ ♦

(On the root of all evil,
  Your popularity depends;
The thicker the bankroll,
  The thicker the friends.)

You can lead your horse to water,
  The result you leave to fate;
Take the same lead with your women,
  The result is whiskey straight.

♦ ♦ ♦

(You see them in every bar-room,
  The boys with self-centered zeal;
Who buy you drinks till you're dizzy,
  But wouldn't slip you a buck for a meal.)

♦ ♦ ♦

As we stumble through existence,
  From the cradle to the hearse,
Not a damn thing ever happens,
  But what could have been much worse.

THE ACE IN THE HOLE

Some time ago,
As a roust to rounders,
I jokingly
Wrote of the yarn,
The ultimate end
Of a wise guy
Was to sleep
In the sucker's barn.

Naught did I think
At that writing,
True words are oft
Spoken in joke;
I contended
The crack-pot who quote it,
Was some Hi-ja-lo
Fresh out of coke.

At the time
I aimed my ambitions
Along one
Particular line;
Determined
To "muscle in" on the rackets,
Be a big shot,
Play the big time.

"Heavy" stuff
Was right up my alley,—
Took to rackets
Like a pig takes to mud;
The tougher the job,
The more thrilling;
Grand larceny
Seemed to flow in my blood.

Huge success
Was crowning my efforts,
Dame Luck held me
Right in her lap;
In my book
A G-man or copper
Was a boob
And a ten-carat sap.

With fair-weather friends
By the thousand,
My drink
The best champagne wine;
Wore a fortune
In glamorous glittery,
"Diamond Spike"
I was tagged at the time.

Lived in luxury
Like a prince in a palace;
Did my road work
In Cadillac cars;
My clothes were
The last word in fashion;
Paid an ace note a throw
For cigars.

This life was
A bowl of cherries,
Soft as taking cakes
From a kid;
Unheeding,
Though I knew it was written,
The rackets . . .
Were doomed for the skid.

Ever searching
For new fields of conquest,
Often traveling
With uncertain goal;
On a wire tapping exploit
In Reno,
Kind fate dealt
An ace in the hole.

For some time
I'd been washed up on women,
Though I could snare
Any number I'd choose;
They all seemed to be
Leaden and lazy,
Hooked on stuff
Or batty from booze.

Now this one,
A stand-out exception,
She fell for my line
With a bang!
A brown-eyed Bambino
Named Toni,
Full of hell
And tougher than whang.

A moll's life
Was cream on her peaches,
My views fit her guild
Like a glove;
The start
Was what the Doc ordered,
Mutual in viewpoints
Bonded with love.

For years she shared
My endeavors,
Right or wrong
She never would squeal;
No going so tough
She'd weaken—
She had nerves
As steady as steel.

As a rule,
A woman "can't take it,"
Will weaken
When put to the test;
Like all rules
Exists the exception,
The little Dago
Stuck out from the rest.

Countless times
She was put on the carpet,
Dealt every degree
Known to the force;
No rousting or threats
Made her weaken,
Defiantly took it
As a matter of course.

Side by side
We hit many a hazard,
In our resolve
To reap by the "rod,"
Each time she showed
Cold-blooded courage,
Without fear of
Man, devil or God.

I recall a rainy night
Near the border,
We were trapped
On an alcohol run;
While I jockeyed the car
Through the cordon,
She let drive
With our typewriter gun.

No sooner had we
Beat their barrier,
With the tommy still hot
'Cross her lap;
She snuggled
Back into the cushions
To resume
Her broken-up nap.

Another time
When fresh out of cabbage,
We decided
On cracking a pete;
Her end was to act
As lookout,
To stall off
The fuzz on the beat.

When I had the job
Half finished,
Was 'most ready
To pour soup in the box;
Down the stem
Floundered a flatfoot,
Shaking doors
And testing the locks.

I quickly stepped
Into position,
To deal him
A rap on the knob;
I could have
Stuck to my knitting,
The Dago
Was right on the job.

Couldn't hear her sales-talk
To that shomus,
As she weeded him
A big cigar;
The arms of the law
Were around her,
As she polished
The points of his star.

I returned to
Peddling my papers;
In half an hour
I'd finished the trick,
Relieving that crate
Of its "cabbage,"
Then scrammed
With the score in my kick.

On reaching the car,
There sat Toni,
Laughing at
Her own little joke;
She was wearing
That cop's gun and buzzer,
And had also
Gone south with his poke.

Without waiting
For questions or answers,
I started the car
With a lurch;
She said: "Take your time,
He's out like a light,
On the steps
Of the Methodist church."

Mere words
Can't express the feeling
I hold for this
Slip of a moll;
To my views
The peak of perfection,
A true stand-by
In the form of a doll.

She trusted my judgment
Completely,
All decisions I made
Were a go;
It was her undying faith
That proved fatal,
I was always
In charge of the dough.

The sages of old
Have contended,
The primrose path
Must eventually end;
Though a bird may
Fly to the heavens,
Sooner or later
It is forced to descend.

Each bad move
Called for another,
Down the financial skids
I did soar;
Dame Luck left me
Flat as a flapjack.
For me,
Tricks weren't walking no more

While trying to
Pry out of the mire;
My diamonds
I had to disburse,
Thinking surely conditions
Were changing,
They were —
From bad to worse.

Every effort I made
Was a failure,
No matter how hard
I would try;
You'd think
I was getting the cold-deck,
From the Boss Gambler,
Who deals from the sky.

Just to add
Salt to my soreness,
While struggling
To gain a new taw,
I was framed and
Placed on probation,
By a biased judge
And Blue Sky law.

At this point
I was 'most to breaking,
I thought
"What the hell is the use
Of continually
Sticking my chin out
And receiving
All kinds of abuse?"

I sorely confessed
To my Toni,
I was about
At the end of my rope,
Had almost completely
Exhausted
All patience
And most of my hope.

I shall never forget
Her reaction —
She rousted me
Half of the night;
By the time
Her raving was over,
You can bet
I was plumb full of fight.

"You put it out;
Now . . . can't you take it?"
Was a plank in the platform
She laid.
"You should squawk
About being downhearted,
After blowing all the dough
That we've made!

"But, win, place and show,
I'm still with you,
No matter how much
I might rave;
They won't see Diamond Spike
Pack the banner,
If I die of old age
On the pave.

"After all these years
As your partner,
Taking the bitter
Along with the sweet,
Do you think
I'll step out of the picture,
And not help you
Back on your feet?

"I'm not moulded from
That make of metal;
We're still pals,
As we've been from the start,
Keeping the vow
We made the Sky-Pilot,
To stick together
Till death do us part.

"I'll play the game
With the ceiling the limit,
Dead willing to
Shake, rattle and roll,
Go any route
That will cart home the 'cabbage,'
And pull you back
Out of the hole.

"This tough luck
Can't hold on forever;
You're in a rut,
But still able to move.
Keep on driving
And trying,
You're bound to hit
Going that's smooth.

"No disgrace
Blowing the bankroll, —
We can get even
In one single bet;
We'll put our nose
To the grindstone;
The tougher it comes,
The tougher we'll get.

"Pull your chin up
Off your chest.
Take the breaks
With a stiff upper lip.
Laugh off
Existing conditions,
Continue to
To stick with the ship.

"It's not like you,
Beefing and squawking,
Wearing a scowl
As black as the night;
I've seen you go down,
A dozen times,
But you would always
Get up and fight.

"You were not cut out
For a quitter,
Or you'd long since
Been riding a hearse;
Don't baby-shoes
Over haywire happenings —
Remember
It could have been worse.

"You're soured up
On the rackets,
And as hot
As a forty-four rod.
You need
A change of scenery,
New environment
And travel strange sod.

"You still have good health,
Thank heaven,
And plenty of guts
To begin
Right back on the creeks
Where you started.
Stay in there
And pitch till you win."

So, I piked right back
To the mountains,
To make or break
On a gold-bearing creek;
Back to the beans
And sour-dough flapjacks,
Back to "the hard way"
With shovel and pick.

It's no bargain
For a "Johnnie-Come-Lately,"
It's tough as hell,
I've been here before;
You can bet
All the rice raised in China,
I'll stick to the creek
Till I score.

You can have my end
Of the rackets;
I'm wound up
Like a bundle of yarn;
You play the part
As the wise guy,
I'll be the sucker
And furnish the barn.

I'll fight my way
Up the ladder,
If I have to pan dirt
Round the Pole,
To make good
For the sake of my Toni —
God bless my little
ACE IN THE HOLE.

THAT GOLD MINER UP YONDER

Did you ever sit a dopin'
Out in the great wide open,
Beside your campfire
After night had gathered 'round;
When the moon across the mountain
Really seemed to be a countin'
All the million little nuggets
Looking down.

Did you ever stop and ponder,
On the paystreak way up yonder,
Not a color
Ever seems to wash away;
The thought got me a goin',
And it kept right on a growin',
Till I think of it
Most every night and day.

That Gold-digger way up yonder,
Must surely be a wonder,
To place them in the bedrock
So they stay;
Yet every night you're gazin',
You'll find them all ablazin',
In the same old place
And in the same old way.

I couldn't help but thinkin',
As I watch them all a blinkin',
If any mug who thinks he's wise
And some to spare;
Would attempt to clean that bedrock
He'd wind up in a headlock,
With that old miner
Who's a runnin' things up there.

TAKE IT AND LIVE IT

A thousand cults
A thousand creeds,
Is one a rose,
The rest all weeds?
Is each one suited
To meet some needs?
Is yours so great
The rest seem small?
Then take it and live it,
That's All.

Buddhist or Christian,
Pagan or Jew,
How do you know
Your own is true,
Not for him or for me,
Or for others, but you,
To live by, to die by,
To stand or to fall,
Then take it and live it,
That's All.

When the strong are cruel,
The weak oppressed,
Will it help you to help,
Will it sing in your breast,
Will it sob in your soul,
With a wild unrest,
Will it fight against might,
Let nothing appall?
Then take it and live it,
That's All.

When the wolves of the world
  Are upon your back,
Does it help you to beat
  The mad horde back,
As you laugh at the snap
  Of the howling pack?
Does it ring in your heart
  Like the huntsman's call?
Then take it and live it,
  That's all.

When your last day comes
  And you take your stand,
And the sword of your strength
  Breaks out of your hand,
And the earth beneath
  Turns to shifting sand,
Will it save you
  When your back's against the wall?
If it does . . . you have it,
  That's all.

MEAT ON THE TABLE OR BUST...

Along the foothills
 Of the Siskiyou Mountains,
Where deer hunters
 Flock thicker than wheat,
Appeared a fat Jew
 From the city,
Hell bent for
 Venison meat.

Pitched his camp
 On the Klamath River,
Near the tavern
 Of Moon Quigley and wife;
Hired "Buckhorn George" Nelson
 To guide him,
As he'd never shot a deer
 In his life.

His makeup . . .
 The last word in huntsware,
Loomed up like
 A flare in a fog;
A Monkey Ward rifle
 And shot-gun,
A Persian cat
 And Pekinese dog.

From the take-off
He amplified ambition,
Early to rise
And seldom late to retire,
Realizing a record run
For his money,
And that the Karok
Well earn his hire.

For weeks
He milled over the foothills,
From crack of dawn
Till late afternoon,
Spending his evenings
Basking in bourbon,
And beefing his bad bargain
To Moon.

Finally, Moon
Raved a rally to the rescue:
"I'll make that redskin
Bite the dust;
And guide you with guarantee,
Come the morrow,
That it's meat on the table
Or bust . . . . "

Early away
Scarce a turn, from the tavern
Moon signaled the Hebrew
To hush,
As he pointed
At something moving
Along the creek,
In back of some brush.

"Take ample aim,"
The able antique advised him,
"Rest your trusty
On the trunk of yon tree,
Aim your shot
For the tip of the shoulder,
Fire fast
For he's afixin' to flee."

The hungry huntsman
Happily heeded,
Down dropped
That mammal of meat;
The fat Kike
Unfamiliar with firearms,
Was also dropped
Flat on his seat.

Moon beat a bold break
For the bushes,
Fast as his limpy legs
Would allow,
In a moment
Hollered harshly to the Hebrew:
"FOR CHRIST'S SAKE! . . . .
YOU'VE SHOT MY OLD COW! . ."

EDUCATED FISH

The reason why
  The fish don't bite,
Like they did
  In days gone by;
They've gone in
  For education,
Is the simple
  Reason why.

Far, far out
  In the blue Pacific,
Where the water
  Is clear and cool;
You'll find young
  Salmon and steelhead
Are attending
  Grammar school.

When they graduate
  From lower grades,
They enroll
  And enter high;
Where they learn
  About the dangers
Of the spinner,
  Spoon and fly.

Then four years of
University,
With its learning
They are set
To duck and dodge
All sorts of lure,
As well as
Spear and net.

Now when they
Journey up the rivers,
With diplomas
'Neath their fins;
They pass
The patient angler by
With long
And knowing grins.

Often drifting in
Quite cautiously,
To look
The tackle o'er;
And comment
On the dumbness
Of us suckers
On the shore.

THE TRUTH, SO HELP ME

There was a pocket hunter,
  Geo. Milne,
As a gold digger,
  Was world renowned;
Once uncovered
  The biggest damn nugget,
Ever garnered
  From gravel or ground.

It was up on
  Indian Girl mountain,
He and Lon Collins,
  Of Double-Jack fame,
Were panning the lead
  To a pocket,
That threw a trace
  Like the wake of the Maine.

One day, Lon
  Delayed at the cabin,
To bake beans
  And sour-dough bread,
When later he ascended
  The diggings,
The sight he saw
  Most knocked him dead.

There was Milne
   Sweating and swearing,
Mucking in mire
   Clean up to his knees;
De-nuding a nugget
   As big as a bucket,
Gold? . . . . Hell, No!
   LIMBURGER CHEESE!

THE CROWD IN THE ROAD

I Disagree with what
  The Poet has said,
Of the House
  By the side of the way;
The Master had neither
  A house nor a home,
He walked with the crowd
  Day by day.

I think when I read
  Of the Poet's desire,
To live in the house
  By the road;
Tolerance is found
  In its tenderest form,
When you walk
  With the crowd in the road.

I say, let me walk
  With the crowd in the road,—
Let me seek out
  The burdens that crush;
Let me speak a kind word
  Of cheer to the weak,
Who have fallen behind
  In the rush.

There's wounds to be healed,
   Breaks we must mend,
A cup of cold water
   To give;
The man in the road
   By the side of his friend,
Is the man
   Who has learned how to live.

Tell me no more
   Of the house by the way,
There's only one place
   I can live;—
It's there with the crowd
   That is milling along,
Needing the cheer
   I can give.

While it's pleasant to live
   In the house by the way,
"Be a friend of man"—
   As the Poet has said;
The Master is bidding:
   "Bear ye their load;
Your rest waiteth
   Yonder ahead."

I could not remain
   In the house by the way,
Idly watching
   The toilers go on;
Their faces beclouded
   With pain and with sin,
So burdened
   Their strength nearly gone.

I'll go to their side,
  Speak in good cheer,
I'll help them
  To carry their load;
And smile at the man
  In the house by the way,
While I walk
  With the crowd in the road.

Out there in the road
  That goes by the house,
Where the Poet
  Is singing his song;
I'll walk and work
  Midst the heat of the day,
And help
  Fallen brothers along.

Too busy to live
  In the house by the way,
Too restless
  For such an abode;
Come rain, hail or snow!
  Win, place and show,
I'll walk
  With the crowd in the road.

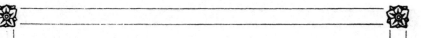

JUST AROUND THE CORNER

Just around the corner,
A stone's throw from here—
Lives a lifelong friend
We hold most dear;
Yet, days go by
And weeks rush on,
Before we know it
A year has gone,
And we have not seen
Our old friend's face;
For life is a
Fleeting, flaming race;
He knows we like him
Just as well
As in the days
We'd ring his bell
And he'd ring ours;
We were younger then,
Now, we are tottering tired men;
Tired of playing
A foolish game,
Tired of struggling
For fortune and fame;
Tomorrow, we say,
Some greeting we'll send
Yes, better still,
We'll call on our friend;

But tomorrow comes
And tomorrow goes,
The distance between us
Grows and grows;
Just around the corner,
Yet years away,
A message! Sir—
"Your Friend died today."
That's what we get
And deserve in the end,
Just around the corner
A neglected friend.

UNSUNG HEROINES

Mothers, we humbly salute you,
For the part you so bravely play
In worldwide struggles for freedom—
In heartaches you silently pay.

The scales are out of balance
In allotments of merit won;
While we sacrifice mere luxuries,
You sacrifice your son.

You keep the homefires burning,
You breath the silent prayer,
When the family sits at mealtime,
And you gaze at that vacant chair.

It's a heavy load, that cross you bear,
For a cause you most abhore;
Mothers all—you stand alone—
Unsung heroines of the war.

PLAY OUT THE STRING

If what you do is wrong or right,
Play out the string!
No goal is gained without a fight,
Play out the string!
Don't alternate your course of play
To hell with what the critics say
If you've got the guts you'll make it pay,
Play out the string!

If the route you choose is icy thin,
Play out the string!
And leads along the path of sin,
Play out the string!
Don't try to cover up or hide,
Tho it calls for social suicide,
Let your conscience be your guide,
Play out the string!

With two strikes on you at the plate,
Play out the string!
A fan-out surely stamps your fate,
Play out the string!
Don't alone on luck your fortune pin,
Nor depend on help from old man gin,
It's up to you to lose or win,
Play out the string!

If reward for labor seems too slow,
Play out the string!
The darkest clouds bring brightest snow,
Play out the string!
Don't haste the harvest of your hay,
Rome wasn't built in a single day,
Stick and stay and whack away,
Play out the string!

When good earth turns to shifting sand,
Play out the string!
Don't weaken wane or tip your hand,
Play out the string!
When roots of effort start to rot,
And all endeavors turn to pot,
Give it everything you've got,
Play out the string!

THAT OLD ACE IN THE HOLE

This town is full of guys,
Who think they're mighty wise;
Just because they know a thing or two;
You can see them every day
Strolling up and down Broadway
Telling of the wonders they can do.

Now there's Conmen and there's Boosters,
Card-sharks and Crapshooters,
They congregate around the Metropole;
They wear fancy ties and collars,
But where they get their dollars,
They all have an ace down in the hole.

Some of them write
To the old folks for coin,
That's their old ace in the hole;
While others have girls
On that old tenderloin;
That's their old ace in the hole;

If you'll listen they'll tell you,
Of trips they're going to make,
From Frisco up to the North Pole,
But their names would be mud,
Like a Chump playing stud,
If they lost that old ace in the hole.

—SUB-CHORUS—

They will tell you of money
That they have made and spent,
And then flash a big bank-roll;
But you'll find them in time,
Standing in that old bread-line,
If they lost that old ace in the hole.

(Editor's note)

By popular request the Author gives you herewith the original words of "That Old Ace in the Hole," written and submitted for copyright April 2nd, 1906.

CONFIDENTIAL ADVICE

When it's your turn at bat,
    Take a cut at the ball;
The bigger they come,
    The harder they fall.

♦ ♦ ♦

Don't be slowed by your appearance,
    Look and act the best you can;
It's true, man makes the clothing,
    The clothes don't make the man.

♦ ♦ ♦

If you go to bat on a caper,
    And figure you might take a fall,
Plead not guilty, call for a jury,
    Select men around six foot tall.

♦ ♦ ♦

Don't weaken when things go hay-wire,
    And you are taking it on the chin;
Cinch up the slack in your Levi's —
    Stay in there and pitch till you win.

♦ ♦ ♦

If you wind up in a jackpot,
    It's the reward for what you've earned;
When you stick your duke in the fire,
    You're damned sure to get it burned.

♦ ♦ ♦

Soft pedal on the broadcasts
    Of things you've done or said;
Three men can keep a secret
    If two of them are dead.

Seek council at all hearings,
    Don't depend on luck or fate;
There's always two strikes on you,
    When you walk up to the plate.

♦ ♦ ♦

That bunk about natural talent
    Is but a gist of idle talk;
We all must learn before we earn,
    And crawl before we walk.

♦ ♦ ♦

If you beef with a native of the Rio Grande
    Better figure all bets as a loss;
Or you may get a Texas Greeting,
    In the spot your suspenders cross.

THE HOMECOMING

As he scraped the last tar
  From the ten spot,
Rolled the pill
  And puffed the pod deep,
Doused the glim
  And straightened the yen-hock.
In fondest fancies
  Of that heavenly sleep;

Quickly stashed the lay-out
  In the Plantsville
Tossed the well-polished card
  To the flames,
Plowing the deep brought
  A dream of attending
The home-coming high-jinks
  Of rounders and dames.

There were conmen,
  Cannons, boosters,
Tipsters, with the race
  In the bag;
Suit-case gamblers
  Men on the heavy,
Creepers, peepers,
  Gals from the drag.

Top shooters, cold deckers
Stallers,
First passers,
Who plank the dough down;
Ladies of leisure,
Fishers and shrimpers,
Howlers, prowlers,
Men-about-town.

Sheetmen, peatmen,
Hi-jackers;
Shakers,
With the federal bluff;
Fainting frailies,
Weepers, leapers,
Muggers, sluggers,
Peddlers of stuff.

Torpedoes,
Who rub out the squeelers;
Bootleggers,
From all points of the land;
Queer passers,
Hypers, kiters,
And a few rodents
From the Rio Grande.

They assembled
In the house-of-all-nations,
In Bartlett Alley,
On the Barbary Coast;
Lee Francis
Was the charming hostess,
Mike the Bite
The genial host.

Coatless Eddie
  Filled the bill as announcer,
Clem McCarthy
  Refereed all the scraps;
Dan Delaney
  Was official gateman,
To bar out
  Sight-seers and saps.

Dick Todd
  And jolly Jack Evershaw
Were in charge
  Of the gaffs near and fars;
Bill Pappas
  Was king of the kitchen,
Al Hoffman
  Dealt out Spanish guitars.

Bar dogs
  In pocketless fiddles,
Frank Gould
  And Parlorhouse Red;
Rosie Bastido,
  Pretty Phil Anderson,
Buddy Harmon
  And Curley the Lead.

Bill Rogers, Harry Waters,
  Jew Farber,
Bob Forrest, Jim Bailey
  And Jack Quinn;
Buff Gargano, Dutch Rath,
  Larry Brennan,
Warren Wilson and
  The "Slap-Happy" Finn.

Singing waiters
    And baritone buss-boys,
Marching in
    With pomp and poise;
Rags Justi, Sam Brown,
    Blackie Morris,
Matt Dromie and
    The Frankovich Boys.

Spike Hennessy, Frosty Jones,
    Harvy Miller,
Geo. Avas, Ace LaMarr
    And Earl Bell;
Scotty Randall, Jake Woitt,
    Billie Stevens,
Fire-cracker Tune, Earl Bush
    And Ted Snell.

A galaxy of
    Gay gorgeous Girlies,
Entertainers
    Of world renown;
Kay Johnson, Tiny Watson,
    Vera St. Peter,
"Duchess" Keys
    And Alaska Babe Brown.

Rita Roberts, Sonny James,
    Nellie Anderson,
Gloria Stewart, Laurine Friend
    And Billie White;
Ethel Sumner, Sadie Shipley,
    Jackie Sherman,
Virginia The Spider
    And Margaret Knight.

Muriel Sherwood, Edna Roberts,
  Geenie Grainger,
Lillie Martin, Penny Davis
  And June Love;
Juanita Dyer, Joyce Barret,
  Vernie Duffy,
Elane Kingston and
  Dottie "The Dove."

Eva Taylor
  Was joe goss of the checkroom,
Ably assisted
  By Bertha the Bum;
Madge Baily
  And Crescent City Jerry
Sold sweet marguerites,
  Peanuts and gum.

Al Blake
  Directed the girl show,
Made up wholly
  Of pink from the pike;
Danny Dennis
  Did stuff on the Steinway,
While Claudie Smith
  Crooned through the mike.

Peanuts Randall
  Manhandled the musicians,
His theme song
  The "Chinatown Blues;"
Jane Jones lulled lyrics
  By her lonesome,
When Mel and George
  Got barreled on booze.

Ed Olson
   Had the roulette concession,
Jimmy House
   The twenty-one snaps;
Jake Hageson
   Old army and faro,
Jack Shalter
   Klondike and craps.

Harry Weaver
   Mucked the pan-inguinge,
The Macgimpers
   All gave it a play;
Joe Conde
   Spun the big six wheel,
Swede Hanson
   Dealt ace a-way.

Early arrivals
   Were Frankie and Johnnie,
Barnacle Bill
   And Sunbonnet Sue;
My Gal Sal
   And Minnie the Moocher,
Willie the Weeper
   And Louieville Lou.

The fish and shrimp
   From the Lehigh Valley,
Blew in
   With a torch in each hand;
Wound up with the
   Ake-ta and bulldog,
Of the girl
   With the Blue Velvet Band.

While the lady known as Lou
  Was posing,
Dan McGrew strolled in
  Through the door,
Caught the Vagabond Kid
  Drawing pictures
Of her face
  On the bar-room floor.

Dan did a high dive
  Through a window,
Like a bob-cat
  Out of its lair;
When in staggered the miner
  Fresh from the creeks,
Dog dirty
  And loaded for bear.

The Ragtime Kid
  Spanked the piano,
As he flopped down there
  Like a fool;
After two sniffs
  From Sam McGee's bindle,
Got reared up
  And fell from the stool.

Nell Streeter
  Dealt 3-card Monte
To Tobe Williams
  And the Kokomo Kid;
Calamity Jane
  Playing strip poker
With Jim Brodie
  And Cripplecreek Sid.

Jerry Murphy
    Mushed in from Alaska
With Klondike Kate
    And Swiftwater Bill;
Bigfoot George
    And Saltpork Mary,
Alaska John
    And Diamond-tooth Lill.

From Fairbanks in
    Mucklucks and Parkas,
Jimmy Cooper
    The Mystery Man;
Bull-dog Cole,
    Billy Gordon "The Couger"
And the Milkovichs,
    Betty and Dan.

The Fairbanks Flash,
    Galloping Freda,
Little Edna
    Plus "Boy-friend" LeRoy;
Dynamite Red and
    Panama Hattie,
Art Hanson,
    The real Alaskan McCoy.

The trimmest trio
    Thumbed in from Chicago,
That ever figured
    To swing from a limb:
The Cicero Kid,
    Alias Mike Garabosi,
Scarfaced Capone
    And Hickory Slim.

From the sumps
  Of New York's subways,
Nickey Arnstein
  And Fifth Avenue Frank;
Bowery Bobbie
  And Onie the Madden,
Tammany Tim
  And Highpocket Hank.

Denver Col
  Sent a truckload of talent:
Figurehead Marty
  And the Yakima Kid;
Lazy Leo Shaw
  And Gloomy Gus Domedian,
Rusty Rusted
  And Larry the Lid.

Rough bottom Shovelers
  From Butte Montana,
Slim Robinson
  And Timberline Tess;
Rocky the Crab
  And One Punch Mooney,
King Richard McLeod
  And Seattle Bess.

From Red Mountain,
  That dot on the desert,
Came Harry Moss,
  The gals' Santa Claus;
Slim LaBorde, Johnnie Raybourn,
  Sis Hopkins,
Big Chief Riffle
  With a squadron of squaws.

Reno Rowdies worth
  Dishonorable mention,
Who for years have been
  Ducking the noose;
Dead Eye Desmond,
  Antone the Frenchman,
Georgie the Hague
  And Sammy Caruse.

Scoop Schlump, Blondy Moore,
  George Dehy,
Felix DeVanni and
  Jimmy the Crab;
Pete the Finn,
  Business Joe Beloso,
Dal Dalrimple and
  Long Shot McNabb.

Big butter and eggmen
  From Portland,
Cactus Jack
  And Johnnie the All;
Oscar Lund,
  Argonaut Casey,
The Baldfaced Kid
  And Harry Duvall.

Skiing in from
  The slopes of Mt. Shasta,
Jack Lutz,
  The big Taxicab Man;
Roy Donaldson,
  Bull S. Montgomery,
Ping Davis, Tiny Booth
  And Jew Anne.

Slick McNeill, Bob Horton,
Dave Penrose,
Kid Scatter,
The Prince of the pike;
Rollie Dahler, Bob Ward,
Carl Dixon,
Vince Galetti and
"Choker-hole" Mike.

From Dunsmuir
Via side-door pullman,
Slim Davis,
A rare piece of goods;
Billy Bascum,
Big Dinny McCauley,
Jack Wyatt and
Dimple Dolly Woods.

Charley Carlquist, Tode Payne,
Mike Padulla,
Flo Montgomery and
Lovin' Larry Jaynes;
Tom Loftus,
"Correll Jim" McGowan,
Cab Reed and
Four dazzling Dames.

Yrekans in a
"B" Twenty-niner,
Pilot Ken Kleaver,
The Demon of Speed,
Co-pilots Red Morris,
Walt Weinrich,
Tail-gunners
Con DeWitt and Ab Weed.

Hitchplaning with
   Liquid luggage,
Rox Cousineau, Jimmy Rae
   And Soldaine;
Shorty Russell, Brownie Slack,
   Ed Conway,
Ever-ready Alton and
   A Youngie Named Jane.

Barbutte Bouncers from
   Weed and Shastina,
Crazy Jerry
   At the helm of the bus;
Jim Davis and
   "Carnivall Mike" Krekos,
The Georges Brothers and
   Psalm-Singing Gus.

The High-roller
   Frank Mussolini,
Tom Sterling and
   Jimmy the Jew;
Chalk Sabarbo, Pete Cunial,
   "Boss" Groppi,
Frank Belcastro and
   Genoa Lounge Lou.

Barging in with
   Shotguns blazing,
Honker hunters
   From Tule Lake;
Bill Seigler, Pewee Stubbs,
   Ray Morosco,
The "Duchess" and
   Roy "Rough-'em-up" Drake.

Embarking from a
  Seagoing whaler,
Modern pirates with
  Insignia spread;
Crewed by Jess Millet,
  Geo. Curtis and Al Falkins,
Ably captained by
  Modoc Red.

Gladiators from
  Ellis and Mason,
Playing Hold 'em
  And Run-up stud;
Crab Smith, Ted Titenger,
  Bill Callero,
The Royal Slav and
  Cliffe "The Galloper" Judd.

Gandy Dancers of
  One Ten Eddy,
Johnnie Pederson and
  Ruby Red Knight,
Chas. Lindeman, Benny Wolfe,
  Duke Dugan,
Pat Patterson and
  Joyous Jerry White.

Johnnie Come Latelies
  And Gay Cabalerros,
Flitting in
  From hither and yon;
Blue Wilsie and
  Baby Face Benson,
The Capri Boys,
  George, Billy and John.

Marco Grant, Ben Norton,
   Don Wollery,
Ren Renshaw and
   Jimmy the Greek;
Sid the Yid, Walt Blake,
   Pete Conley,
Jimmy Levan and
   Ed Silva "The Shiek."

Billy Lott quite at home
   At the Hammond,
Rendering music that
   Soothes the soul;
Busher Thornton brot
   Applause most deafening,
As he sang
   "That Old Ace in the Hole."

Red Hogan
   Started his stud game
Six for two
   And a split of the win;
Billy Muir
   Gave him a fast one,
Bought a stack
   With a counterfeit finn.

Mack Smith
   Shook the box razzle-dazzle,
With Scarface Murphy
   And Jimmy the Goat;
Society Red
   Put his shiv into action,
When Jack Dalton
   Tried to lay him the note.

Mable Hoppy
    Decked out in simples,
Cutting up touches
    With Titanic Slim;
Babe Meister
    Dishing dirty stories
To Nick the Greek
    And Three-Finger Jim;

Roy De Money dealing
    No limit faro,
To Curly Bittrick, Peachart
    And Bum Spears;
George Gainer, Doubleup,
    Blackie Disney,
Skinny Anderson, St. Louis Dutch
    And Joe Mears.

While Beda Leddy
    Was doing a fan dance,
The Swede Kid
    Put on the peek;
Anita Mitchell
    Sang Frankie and Johnnie
To Bert the Barber
    And Jerry the Greek.

Big Darby Con,
    The Shiek of Sacto,
Incited
    A hilarious riot,
Barging in
    With a singer's midget,
Claiming his doctor
    Had ordered a diet.

Ford Myers
  In full dress regalia,
The Boob Kid
  Stewed to the ears,
Sammy Corenson
  With his trusty tapeline,
Measuring gals
  For furlined brassieres.

Coffee Klotzing
  In the Two Dollar Parlor,
Gefiltefish and shoptalk
  Held sway;
Sammy Good, Jew Bess
  And Annie Adler,
The Foster's gang
  And Kentucky May.

Rough House Newton,
  Rooting for trouble,
Fighting Red Graham
  Was calling his bluff;
The Blue Ribbon Special
  Threw a whing-ding,
While Deep Diving Dick
  Was strutting his stuff.

Violet Wilson
  Singing a torch song
To Jack McLean
  And Abrams Boy Sid;
Hazel Green
  Dancing the hula
For Earl Wallace
  And the Cherokee Kid.

Crying Johnnie
  Moaning and groaning
On the shoulder
  Of Salvation Nell,
Charlie Sly
  And Big Tar-baby
Knocked him off
  With a pea and a shell.

On the dance floor
  Doing the big apple,
Dago Mary
  And Abie the Jew,
Tow Boat Annie
  And Two-Step Kelly,
The Dancing Kid
  And Singapore Sue.

Tonopah Kelley
  Caught his thumb in the holdout
Trying to cold deck
  Montana Rose,
When Nevada May
  Did a strip tease cantata,
Freddie Baggs
  Powdered out with her clothes.

Doing a fair job
  At tipping the tiddlies,
Clara Williams
  And Steve the Stew,
Silent Dick Charters
  And Rough House Mary,
Clifford the Young
  And Beer Barrel Sue.

Al Heil
   Shed tears big as teacups,
As Bobbie Burroughs
   Sang "Mother Machree,"
The Oregon Apple
   Got a whack on the whiskers
For copping a feel
   From Spanish Marie.

Marco the Mogul
   Making a pep talk
To June Taylor
   And Peggy Mahone;
Gold Highbaum
   Had to call up and Punchville,
And was hustling a slug
   For the phone.

Chief performers
   In a jitterbug contest—
Bible Moreno
   And Taxicab Jean;
The Oakland Champ
   Walter Bailey,
Freddy Kelly
   And Conchita the Queen.

Lard Bottle Price,
   Jack Shinn, Joe Brantley,
Pesty Clark
   And Louie the Louse
Were enjoying the party
   Immensely,
As the tids
   Were on the rat and mouse.

Josephus Bailey,
  The pride of Peoria,
Playing pinochle
  With Jimmy the Fid;
Herb Bell
  Teaching the rhumba
To Nellie Moor
  And the Necktie Kid.

Pussyfoot
  Was mooching a cuter,
To buy a bindle
  From Panhandle Pete;
Smokey Joe
  Got tossed in the bucket
For taking a sunday
  At the cop on the beat.

Playing pan
  At a back cane and able,
Bill Alvarado
  And Pete the Swede;
Slicker Slim Jones
  And Lantern-jaw Kelly,
The Gabby Barber
  And Jimmy the Weed.

Dolly Fine
  Was barred at the barrier,
And flew into a most
  Furious rage,
When she showed up
  With four college students
Who were much, . . too much,
  Under age.

While French Louie
  Was mixing a Mickey,
In the thick and thin
  Of Whitey Markell,
Nate the Cot
  Switchvilled the tiddlies,
And Louie
  Beat Paddock's time all to hell.

Curbstone Banks
  Was late in arriving —
Claimed his tire
  Had picked up a nail
Near the corner
  Of Powell and Market,
While trolling
  For San Quentin quail.

Checks Sloan
  Got greasy and grimy,
Mining for luck money
  Under the rugs,
But was barred
  From using the bathtub,
As Blondy Seaton
  Had pilfered the plug.

Giving "Sweet Adeline"
  A fair going over,
Mickie Springer
  And Monterey Grace,
Stuttering Sam
  Was crooning the tenor,
Jimmie McKay
  Played a swell second base.

Farmer Page
    Passed out of the picture,
In the chalk farms
    Of Sally the Soak—
Crooked Arm Goldie
    Clouted his wristwatch,
Raz Jones
    Sneezed his tie pin and poke.

Bone Head Remmer
    Dealt high-limit blackjack
To the "IT" girl
    Of Hollywood fame,
But she paid off
    With readers of rubber,
Claiming the cheques
    Were as good as the game.

Patty Mullen
    Threw two sixes as usual,
Wound up
    With a bump on the bean,
For sticking toothpicks,
    Smeared in mustard,
Into the whiskers
    Of Man-Mountain Dean.

An S.O.S. call
    Came from a shovel,
Nick Walters
    Had beaten the gate,
Horned in
    On a petting party
Between Gene Davis
    And Salt Lake Kate.

Handsome Bill Irish,
God's gift to women,
Percolating
As big as you please,
Till the Cheese and Kisses
Appeared unexpected,
Caught him necking
With Cock-eyed Louise.

Red Ray
Called up from the bastile,
He and Olcott
Had been on a lark,
And wound up
In the arms of the enemy
For shooting swans
In Golden Gate Park.

As Dutch White
Sang "The Last Rose of Summer,"
Silvers McGuire
Gave lusty Bronx cheers;
Big Rosie
Got a slap on the kisser
For snatching
Billy the Bum by the ears.

In a three cushion
Billiard contest,
For the elite
Of the racetrack clan,
Kyne and Normile
Were dead-heat winners,
While Slip Madigan
Also ran.

Narrow Gauge Bond
   And Simon Legree Sullivan,
Big shots
   Of Reno's tavern of luck,
Were worried sick
   That during their absence
Some shill
   Would go south with a buck.

Vern Shannon,
   The Clark Creek two-gun-man,
Demonstrating
   His archery stance;
Eddie Roberts
   Played a saxophone solo,
While Frank Leddy
   Did a buck and wing dance.

Playing low ball
   With a buck and a bottle,
The Morman Kid
   And Broken Nosed Joe,
Bennie Chapman
   And Slippery Slim Gordon,
Sacramento Butch
   And Little Jockie LeBow.

The mayor of Chinatown,
   Sad as a salmon,
Had just blown
   His ace in the hole —
While clouting a light bulb
   From the toilet,
His toupee
   Skidded into the bowl.

Seattle Jew Mike,
  Dave Wired and Ben Silver,
Playing call-shot
  For a "C note" a frame —
Blonde Helen
  Went south with the eight ball,
And they were unable
  To finish the game.

Fog Horn Murphy
  Holding a conference
With Gus Oliva
  And Panama Frank,
Laying plans
  For copping some cabbage
From the First National
  Handle and crank.

Slot Machine Johnnie
  Bet a grand on the Derby,
Baroni's entry
  To run in the dough —
Pinkey Bell
  Laid it six, two and even,
Billie Lee
  Bet a deuce on the show.

Sam Barbour,
  Famed scribe of the Read Head,
Was on hand
  For a scoop of the news;
Billy Giff
  Took a poke at Dan Gorden
For hot-footing
  The sole of his shoes.

A battle royal
Was staged in the kitchen
Between Dinty Moore
And Hamburger Jim,
Coffee Dan and
"T" Bone Riley,
Chicken Charley
And Slaughterhouse Slim.

The bathing beauty contest
Was a riot,
But ended up
In a saddened surprise —
Before the judges
Could make their decision,
Blondy Herron had
Joe Halled with the prize.

A main event
Was held in the open.
On the lot
Where they park the machines,
Between Jack Dempsey,
That grand old mauler,
And Gentleman Gene,
Of the fighting Marines.

Jack lowered the boom
In the seventh,
The leatherneck swan-dived
To the floor;
Joe Soap
Took a kick at his darby,
And McCarthy counted
To a hundred and four.

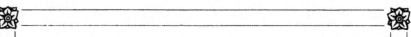

The best bet of the day
Was the banquet,
The Joe Goss
Had so generously supplied.
Hot tamales
Were served on the halfshell,
With a dash of Miller's hash
On the side.

After lunch they did a Sousa
To the basement;
Harry Canama
Spread craps on the floor;
A Texas fink
Blew a buck and yelled copper,
And the Fuzz
Was breaking down the door.

The commotion awakened
The hop head —
Quickly realized
His dream was all spent,
And the pounding on the door
Was the landlord,
Squawking like hell
For his rent.

CHIPS FROM THE DIAMOND

There's sound logic in this adage,
  Not mere chance remarks;
"The truest friend you'll ever have,
  Walks on four feet and barks."

Take a lesson from the salmon,
  That swims in sound and sea;
He opens up and closes up,
  But not a word says he.

There's one born every minute,
  I neither "yes it" nor deny it;
Barnum should have added, that
  They might go on a diet.

A duck you can take from the heavens
  By display of delusive decoy;
A boy, you can take from the country,
  The country, you can't take from the boy.

Every little bit added to what you've got
  Makes just a little bit more;
An apple a day keeps the doctor away,
  It don't keep the wolf from the door.

Dictators may come, dictators may go,
  Flaring forth with flags unfurled;
The hand that rocks the cradle
  Is the hand that rules the world.

A rolling stone gathers no moss,
  We are so reminded every hour;
If it weren't for the rolling stones,
  Where the hell'd we get our flour.

The rich get the gold and silver,
  The poor the stones and sticks;
But when Gabriel starts his one-man band,
  They're all in the same damn fix.

A longer lease on life,
  We can neither beg nor borrow;
Although we're here today,
  We may be gone tomorrow.

You can make a mountain of a mole hill,
  No fox can be made of a fool;
A man, from a ringtailed monkey,
  Or a racehorse out of a mule.

Though women are called the weaker sex,
  For the way they primp their locks;
There's more real strength in a strand of her hair,
  Than there is in a full grown ox.

(In the life partner you choose
  Great care you should use,
If contentment you would attain;
  To each road that leads to happiness,
There's fourteen that lead to pain.)

(To whomever your secret
  You may choose to tell;
You have sold your freedom
  Just as sure as hell.)

Hew your route as fate directs you,
  Let the chips fall where they may;
And all along life's journey
  Live and let live by the way.

THE SUMMARY

Summing up
  My life's ramifications,
I've played the game
  From beginning to end;
Never coughed up my guts
  To a copper,
Copped a plea
  Or turned rat on a friend.

Followed no special line
  Of endeavor,
Any angle
  That would garner the pay,
Without preference
  I stuck to the standard:—
When you find a farmer,
  Harvest his hay.

Put the rackets
  To the tests of the acid,
Worked first class
  Without favor or fear,
From robbing rattlers
  To lifting a leather,
Peddling gilt bricks
  To passing the queer.

Played the con-game
From New York to Frisco,
From the frozen North
To the Mexican coast;
Steering mark after mark
To the clippers,
Who took the play
As their butter and toast.

The largest clip I recall
Was in Brooklyn —
Steered a Hoosier
From Hickory Ridge;
Sold the rhube
Real right and title
To that world-famous
Brooklyn bridge.

Turned another fair trick
Out in Denver,
Through the help
Of a hustler named Flint;
Sold a son of the soil
From Sioux City,
Half interest
In the government mint.

I booted the ball
Once in Frisco,
Mistaking John-law
For a mark —
Tried to peddle
A plain clothes shomas
The band of sheep
In Golden Gate Park.

Thence a memorable sojourn
  In Reno,
Against the elite
  Of the gambling lore;
Posing two years
  As Elmer Squarejohn,
To put over
  A racetrack score.

Became a trusted employee
  Of the company
Who rendered service
  Direct from the track;
What a headache it was
  To those bookies,
As one by one
  They rushed to the rack.

Prohibition was duck soup
  To the rackets,
Soft as picking pods
  From a pond;
Made a barrel of bees
  Out of Bourbon
Hijacked
  From government bond.

But, easy come, easy go,
  Fits the rackets
Like a four-in-hand
  Fits to a collar,
The dough you derive
  For your efforts
Isn't worth a thin dime
  On the dollar.

It seems there's a curse
   On the cabbage
Commonly called
   Illegitimate gain;
Although you make a few grand
   On a caper,
The blow-off
   Is invariably the same.

Oft' times you wind up
   In the bucket.
In this spot
   You're doomed to defeat;
So, you dole off your dough
   To the fixers,
To place your plates
   Back on the street.

Here's a duke
   I would deal young hoodlums:
You were born
   Thirty years too late,
To prosper along the lines
   Of small rackets,
For you'll end up
   In back of the eight.

My experience proves true
   The old saying,
Bro't to mention
   Every hour of the day;
It's the writing on the wall
   To petty rackets —
Those three words:
   "Crime doesn't pay."

It's the small fry
   Society censures,
Not the big shots
   Who play the big time;
If you must be a thief,
   Be a banker;
The larger the score,
   The lesser the crime.

If I had my life
   To live over,
And could turn back
   The pages of time,
I'd hoist sail
   On the sea of religion —
It's more lucrative
   And a less hazardous line.

As it is,
   I'll stick to the standard,
Till they start shoveling
   Dirt in my face;
Tho father time has me
   Tied at the eighth pole,
I'll still give him
   A hell of a race.

It's the thrill of the game
   That I'm wanting,
More than cornering
   The coin of the realm;
When my crime ship
   Sinks into the salty,
I'll go down
   With both hands on the helm.

I recently
  Returned to the "hard way"
With good intent
  And well meaning vow,
To follow the life
  Of a square-john,
Earning bread
  By the sweat of my brow.

Backtracking my trail
  To the mountains,
Filed on a claim
  And built a log shack;
Like the return
  Of the prodigal son,
With open arms
  I was welcomed back.

After two years
  Of mucking and miring,
Was successful
  In procuring the pay,
But a genuine
  Mexican stand-off,
In my adoption
  Of the square-john's way.

Their tactics and deeds
  And unmoral creeds,
Would drive Harry Tracy
  To flight;
They "God bless, Amen" you
  By daylight,
"God damn" and hijack you
  By night.

The merchant and teacher,
  Postmaster and preacher,
All have the same adage
  In view;
Pour the harpoon
  To thy neighbor,
Ere thy neighbor
  Can pour it to you!

I've lived in the
  Censured environment,
From the Bowery
  To the Barbary Coast;
When it comes
  To licentious larceny,
They have gangdom
  Tied to a post.

I turn in my tools
  As a square-john,
I'm washed up
  With this venomous scum;
I'll cop to the plea:
It's too rotten for me;
Honest old underworld,
  Here I come.

You take the gold
  In "them thar mountains,"
Muck in the mire
  Till you break your back;
If you leave with over
  Ass and elbows,
I'll double
  The size of your stack.

There's a sucker
   Born every minute
Quoth old Barnum
   In bravadic blair;
He was right
   And that selfsame sucker
Is any man
   That deals on the square.

For last Christmas
   I'll give you the hard way,
And all the gilt
   You gain from the creeks;
I'll switch back
   To honorable rackets,
Matching wits
   With shisters and dicks.

Adios,
   Mr. Psalm-Singing Square-john,
I'll meet you in the city
   Some day;
You can bet
   All the beans baked in Boston
That I'll knock you in
   For your hay.

Orchids,
   To the racketeers and rounders,
The All-American
   Is back in the ring,
To dish you out
   Fair competition;
Come what may,
   I'll play out the string.

Poison ivy,
To you cutors and coppers;
For your info
I'm pleased to inform —
Until old age
Rings down my curtain,
Never again
Will I attempt to reform.

I gave the square stuff
Honest effort,
Played the game quite
According to Hoyle;
A square plug
Don't fit a rounded hole,
And you cannot mix
Water with oil.

Gone too far
To backtrack or weaken,
It's my beef
If I fall for a frame;
I'll ride the golden rule
Of the rackets,
When you gain the name,
Garner the game.

At the blow-off
I'll cakewalk to heaven,
Cut St. Peter the cards
For my stay;
Slip a Micky Finn
To Old Gabriel,
If he trys to horn in
On my play.

GLOSSARY

and

SLANG LANGUAGES

of the

UNDERWORLD

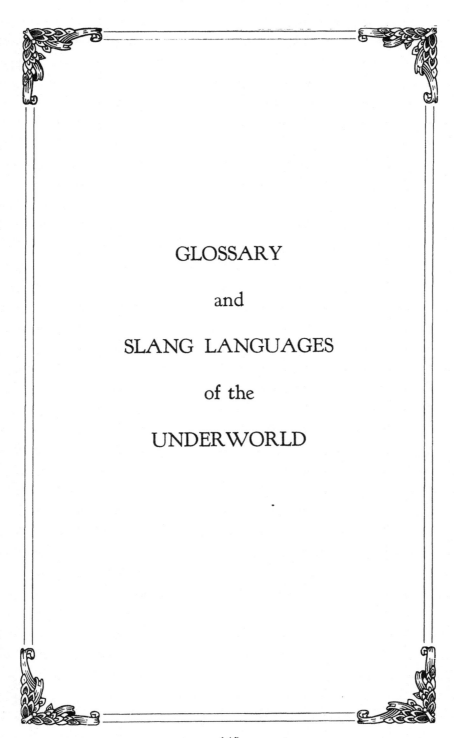

Aketa .... Tainted Money
Ace Away .... Dice Game
Ace Note .... Dollar

Banged .... Doped Up
Baby Shoes .... Lament
Blue .... Negro
Blow .... Loose
Bounce .... Spend
Buck the Tiger .... Gamble
Button .... Money
Big Six .... Gambling Wheel
Bindle .... Package of Dope
Barbaute Bouncer .... Gambler
Bucket .... Jail
Beat the Gate .... Sneak In
Bronx Cheers .... Poops
Brazillians .... Nuts
Big Time .... Big Money Racket
Buzzer .... Police Star
Blue Sky Law .... Kangaroo Court
Boosters .... Thieves
Barreled .... Drunk
Butter and Toast .... Host
Boot the Ball .... Mistake
Bees .... Money
Beef .... Squawk

Carry the Torch .... Be Brokenhearted
Cheno .... Chinaman
Cake .... Money
Can .... Nest Egg
Copy .... A Piece
Cat Hop .... Last Turn-In Faro
Cop a Feel .... Paw

Cuter .... Quarter
Conmen .... Confidence Racketeers
Cannon .... Pick Pocket
Crate .... Safe
Cabbage .... Money
Cheese and Kisses .... The Mrs.
Cold Deck .... Stacked Deck
Crossroaders .... Traveling Cheaters
Cough Up .... To Tell
Cop A Plea .... Plead Guilty
Con Game .... Confidence Racket
Clipper .... Collector
Clip .... Collection
Creeper .... Thief
Chain Stable .... Several Girls

Duke .... Hand
Double Harness .... Team Work
Darby .... Belly
Douced .... Put Out
Drag .... Street
Dicks .... Detectives

Fuzz .... Police
First Passer .... Cinch Bettor
Fish and Shrimpers.................... Pimps
Fainting Frailies .... Female Fainters
Faro .... Gambling Game
Finn .... Five Dollar Bill
Fixers .... Go Between
Framed .... Connived Against
Fiddles .... Suits
Flounder .... Pimp

Grab the Glue .... Get the Money

Go South	Steal
Glim	Lamp
Gaff	A Place
Grand	Thousand
Gilt	Gold
Hijalo	Dope Fiend
Heavy Stuff	Big Rackets
Hardway	Honest Work
Howlers	Squawkers
Hijackers	Thieves
Hypers	Short-changers
High Pitch	To State
Hip Hurrah	Wised Up
High Roll	Bet High
Hold Out	Mechanical Device
Handle and Crank	Bank
Hotfoot	Paper Match
Hay	Money
Info	Information
Joe Goss	Boss
Johnnie Come Lately	Green-Horn
Jug	Jail
Joe Halled	Ran Out With
Knob	Head
Kick	Pocket
Kiters	Check Raisers
Kip	Bed
Kopeck	Dollar
Keester	Suit Case
Klondike	Dice Game
Kane and Able	Table

Leaded .... Sluggish
Ladies of Leisure .... Sporting Women
Leapers .... Bail Jumpers
Lay-Out .... Smoker's Equipment
Lower the Boom.. Hit
Low Ball .... Poker
Lean and Fat.. Hat
Leather .... Purse

Muscle In .... Break Into
Moll .... Gangster's Girl
Men on the Heavy.................... Stickup-Men
Men About Town.......................... Rounders
Muggers .... Photographers
Macgimpers .... Pimps
Melborne Piers .... Queers
Mark .... Sucker
Mexican Standoff...... Lose Money, Save Life

Near and Far.. Bar

Old Army .... Chuck A Luck

Pete .... Safe
Pave .... Sidewalk
Pill .... Portion of Opium
Peepers .... Spotter
Plantsville .... Hideout
Prowler .... Thief
Peteman .... Safe Blower
Peddler .... Dope Seller
Pink .... Young Girl
Pike .... Street
Powdered .... Left
Pappas .... Greek

Plow the Deep	Sleep
Pack the Flag	Down and Out
Pad the Shoe	Get the Money
Pan-inguinge	Card Game
Pasteboards	Cards
Peek	Look
Pea and Shell	Shell Game
Powder Out	Left
Punchville	Report
Pan	Pan-inguinge
Pass the Queer	Counterfeit
Plates	Feet
Play Out the String	From Now On
Queer Passers	Counterfeiters
Roadwork	Travel
Rod	Gun
Rodents	Rats
Rattlers' Hisses	Kisses
Razzle Dazzle	Dice Game
Rat and Mouse	House
Readers	Checks
Rattler	Train
Rush to the Rack	Go Broke
Rough Bottom Shovelers	Shaftmen
Stuff	Dope
Soup	Nitro Glycerine
Stem	Street
Shomus	Policeman
Score	Gain
Sky Pilot	Preacher
Stashed	Hid
Stallers	Cannon's Aid

Sheetman	Policy Salesman
Shaker	Law Impersonator
Slugger	Knockout Thief
Squeeler	Informer
Spanish Guitars	Cigars
Sweet Marguerites	Cigarettes
Sour Score	Bad Gamble
Shovel	Room
Starlings	Girls
Snare a Second	Deal Number Two
Shiv	Knife
Simples	Diamonds
Slug	Phoney Coin
Sunday	To Sock
San Quentin Quail	Young Girls
Shyster	Crooked Attorney
Squarejohn	Honest Man

Typewriter Gun	Machine Gun
Tommy	Machine Gun
Tar	Opium
Ten Spot	Opium Container
Tipster	Tout
Top Shooter	Diceman
Torpedo	Gunman
The Talent	Wise Guys
Take	Cash Receipts
Top of the Box	Start of Faro Game
Take by Mail	Receipts by Mail
Thesies and Thosies	Clothes
Tops	Crooked Dice
Twist	Girl
Tagged	Named
Twenty-One Snaps	Blackjack Games
Tiddlies	Drinks

Thick and Thin.......................................Gin
Turned Rat.........................Double-Crossed

Under Wraps...............................Easy Win

Weepers.......................Professional Cryers
Weeping Willow................................Pillow
Wise Willies...........................Smart Guys
Warbled.. Informed

Yen Hock...........................Opium Holder

THE UNDERWORLD SLANG

Ankle	Barney Frankle
Ale	Pink and Pale
Arm	Chalk Farm
Ass	Bottle and Glass
Bank	Handle and Crank
Back	Sag and Sack
Bail	Hammer and Nail
Bar	Near and Far
Barber	Syndey Harber
Bed	Roses Red
Beer	Oh My Dear
Belt	Feather and Felt
Belly	Darby Kelly
Boots	Daisy Roots
Bottle	Engineer's Throttle
Boss	Joe Goss
Breast	Hornet's Nest
Blink	Pen and Ink
Car	Rumble and Jar
Cab	Jostle and Jab
Cannon	River Shannon
Cap	Bum Wrap
Cashdrawer	Damper and Scamper
Chin	Andy McGinn
Chair	Vanity Fair
Cigar	Spanish Guitar
Cigarette	Sweet Marguerite
Chain	Loss and Gain
Church	Kirkley Birch
Clothes	These and Those

Coat.. Ivory Float
Collar................................Hoop and Holler
Coppers.........................Bottles and Stoppers
Cook......................................Sandy Hook
Colts (Gun)........................Nuts and Bolts
Chink......................................Willin Fink
Check......................................Oh By Heck

Dance.................................Prod and Prance
Daughter..........................Bread and Water
Dice......................................Nits and Lice
Diamond..............................Simple Simon
Dollar.....................................Paper Collar
Drink......................................Tidley Wink
Drunk..............................Elephant's Trunk

Ear...................................Quaint and Queer
Eyes...Mince Pies

Face..............................Lavender and Lace
Fairy....................................Cash and Carry
Feet.....................................Plates of Meat
Finger..............................Long and Linger
Flowers...................................Happy Hours
Folks...Joe Doaks
Frock..................................Rustle and Rock

Gin......................................Thick and Thin
Girl.....................................Twist and Twirl
Gloves...................................Turtle Doves
Glass......................................Scottish Lass
Gun..Hit and Run

Hair...................................Maiden's Prayer
Hands..Iron Bands

Hat....................................Lean and Fat
Head....................................Lunk of Lead
Heel....................................Squirm and Squeel
Hip....................................Lover's Lip
Host....................................Butter and Toast
House....................................Rat and Mouse

Ice....................................Once or Twice
Ill....................................Jack and Jill

Jam....................................Eggs and Ham
Jaw....................................Point of Law
Jail....................................Moan and Wail
Jew....................................Kidney Stew
Judge....................................Candy Fudge

Kiss....................................Rattler's Hiss
Kid....................................God Forbid
Knife....................................Staff of Life

Law....................................Gee and Haw
Legs....................................Mumbly Pegs
Letter....................................Irish Setter
Lips....................................Snake's Hips
Loan....................................Grumble and Groan
Love....................................Heavens Above

Man....................................Heap O' Coke
Money....................................Bees and Honey
Mouth....................................North and South
Mustache....................................Whip and Lash
Mrs....................................Cheese and Kisses

Neck....................................Hurricane Deck
Nigger....................................Jig and Jigger

Nose...I Suppose
Nuts ....Brazillian Huts

Pimp..................................Fish and Shrimp
Pillow...............................Weeping Willow
Pin.......................................Satan and Sin
Pipe...............................Mellow and Ripe
Pocket.....................................Sky Rocket
Poke......................................Oxen's Yoke
Prostitute...........................Boat and Oar

Queer.....................................Melborn Pier

Ring......................................Apron String
Room..............................Shovel and Broom

Rug.......................................Crockery Jug

Shave...............................Rant and Rave
Shine.........................Whimper and Whine
Shirt..Dickey Dirt
Shoes..............................Ones and Twos
Socks..Oscar Hox
Sleep..................................Plow the Deep
Street...............................Fields of Wheat
Stare..................................Gun and Glare
Suit..................................Fiddle and Flute
Sucker ....Elmer Tucker

Table................................Cain and Abel
Take..............................Shiver and Shake
Teeth...........................Upper and Beneath
Tie...Lambs Fry
Thief.......................................Coral Reef
Tits....................................Brace and Bits
Trousers.......................Charley Rousers

Train..Rattle and Rain
Toe..To and Fro
Vest...East and West
Waiter.......................................Fried Potater
Water...........................Mother and Daughter
Wife....................................Storm and Strife
Wine...Silk and Twine
Wrist...Morning Mist
Yellow..................................Meek and Mellow

RACKETEERS

Baggage Thief	Keisterman
Bank Robber	Jug Rooter
Bail Jumper	Leaper
Bottom Dealer	Sumpman
Car Thief	Whip
Check Raiser	Kiter
Check Passer	Paperhanger
Card Mechanic	Ladderman
Confidence Game	Big Store
Counterfeiter	Queerpasser
Confidenceman	Grifter
Carnival Hustler	Carnie
Cold Decker	Switchman
Crap Shooter	Top Shooter
Conman's Collector	Clipper
Cannon Mob	Whiz
Cannon's Aid	Staller
Dope Merchant	Peddler
Drunk Robber	Lush Roller
Female Dip	Whizmoll
Forger	Penman
Gambling Cheater	Sharp Shooter
Gangster's Doctor	Croaker
Gunman	Triggerman
Gangster	Goofer
Heister	Rooter

Killer .... Torpedo
Knockout Thief .... Slugger
Kidnapper .... Snatcher

Liquor Thief .... Hijacker
Law Impersonator .... Shaker
Locater .... Caser

Nitro Expert .... Soupman

Pickpocket .... Cannon
Photographer .... Mugger
Phoney Policyman .... Sheetman
Prostitute .... Swinging Door
Pointer .... Fingerman
Poke Lifter .... Wire
Pimp .... Fisherman
Phoney Stone Peddler .... Iceman
Phoney Parson .... Deacon

Pool Hustler .... Chisler

Queer Shaker .... Muzzler

Room Thief .... Doorshaker
Racetrack Tout .... Tipster
Residence Thief .... Prowler
Robbery Staller .... Fainter

Safe Cracker .... Peteman
Stickupman .... Heavy
Petty Store Thief .... Booster
Short-Change Man .... Hyper
Sleeper-Robber .... Creeper
Sympathetic Cryer .... Weeper
Second Story Man .... Porch-Climber

Shoplifter.. Derrick
Traveling Hustler..............................Suitcaser
Traveling Cheater......................Cross-Roader

Underworld Attorney..........................Shyster

Woman's Purse Thief..................Moll-Buzzer
Waiter.. Spud
Woman Pickpocket........................Whizmoll

NITS AND LICE

Two	Snake Eyes
Three	For Me
Four	Little Joe
Five	Fever in the South
Six	Jimmy Hix
Seven	The Devil
Eight	Katie Bar the Gate
Nine	Long Liz from Boston
Ten	Big Dick
Eleven	Gift from Heaven
Twelve	Mid-Night

BEES AND HONEY

One Cent	Sou Marque
Five Cents	Jitney
Ten Cents	Short Bit-Deemer
Twelve and Half Cents	Bit
Fifteen Cents	Long Bit
Twenty Cents	Twenty Hundred
Twenty-Five Cents	Cuter
Fifty Cents	Half a Man
Seventy-Five Cents	Six Bits
Dollar (silver)	Iron Man
Dollar (paper)	Frog Skin
Dollar Quarter	Buck and Squirt
Dollar Fifty	Cow and a Calf
Two Dollars	Deuce
Two Fifty	Deuce and Four
Five Dollars	Finnan Haddie
Ten Dollars	Saw Buck
Twenty Dollars	Double Saw
Fifty Dollars	Half a "C"
Seventy-Five Dollars	Six Furlongs
Hundred Dollars	Century
Thousand Dollars	Grand
Million Dollars	"M"
Paper Money	Scratch
Silver	Babbit
Gold	Gilt
Checks	Readers
Travelers Checks	A. B. A.
Money Orders	Mo's

BOTTLES & STOPPERS

Amateur Detective	Tin Star
Police Force	John Law
Any Policeman	Copper, Fuzz, Shomus
Police in Uniform	Harness Bulls
Police in Plain Clothes	Elbows
Traffic Police	Corner Clown
Police in Squads	The Enemy
Motorcycle Squad	Bicyclers
Beat Policeman	Flatfoot
Police Horseback	Mounties
Detective	Dick, Nose
Detective Disguised	Gum Shoe
Police in Autos	Cruisers
Special Police	Pinks
U. S. Detectives	Feds
Police in a Raid	Wrecking Crew
Police Investigators	Snoopers
Police Informers	Eries
Police Agent	Fence
Police Go-Between	Fixer
Police Collector	Juice Man
Police Protection	Juice
Dishonest Policeman	Right John
Park Policeman	Sparrow
Bunco Detail	Brain Trust
Stickup Detail	Heavy Squad
Pickpocket Detail	Whizdicks
Private Dick	Eye
Constable	Whittler
F. B. I.	G-Men
Night Watchman	Hack
Honest Policeman	No Record

CODE OF THE CANNON

Pickpocket	Cannon
To Operate	Grift
Working Places	Spots
Church	Kirk
Crowd	Tip or Press
Bank	Jug
Train	Rattler
Street Car	Short
Cab	Jerk
Theatre	Flimsy
Prizefight	Cauliflower
Picnic	Basket Spread
Football Game	Scramble
Baseball Game	Strikeout
Circus	Barnum
Lecture	Gab
County Fair	Rube's Delight
Wrestling Match	Grunt
Department Store	Five and Ten
Elevator	Lift
Sidewalk	Stem Grift
Opening Night	Premier
A Boat	Tub Touch
Racetrack	Stretch
Prospect	Bates
Prospect with Luggage	Kestermark
Prospect on Streetcar	Crosstowner
Chinaman	Original
Jap	Mustard
Foreigner	Hunkie
Amateur Pickpocket	Dig
Italian	Guinea

Negro	Jig
Jew	Pork
Purse Lifter	Wire
Jostler	Staller
Carrier	Pratman
Locating Poke	Fan
Left Front Pants Pocket	Left Britch
Right Front Pants Pocket	Right Britch
Left Hip Pants Pocket	Left Prat
Right Hip Pants Pocket	Right Prat
Trouser Watch Pocket	Block Jerv
Outside Vest Pocket	Jerv
Inside Vest Pocket	Insider
Inside Coat Pocket	Pit
Left Outside Coat Pocket	Left Coat Tail
Right Outside Coat Pocket	Right Coat Tail
Upper Outside Coat Pocket	Rag Pit
Tie Pin	Prop
Watch	Block
Chain	Anchor
Ring	Hoop
Necklace	Rope
Bracelet	Cuff
Knife	Shiv
Keys	Screws
Spectacles	Googs
Handkerchief	Wipe
Cigarettes	Fag Pack
Pipe	Stinker
Tobacco Can	PA
Bank Book	Jug Book
Purses	Leathers
Miner's Purse	Poke
Snap Purse	Tweezer
Long Snap Purse	Shoemaker

Folding Purse .... Accordian
Bill Fold .... Folder
Clip .... Clamp
Money in Handkerchief .... Bundle
Handbag Purse .... Straphanger
Gold .... Ridge
Small Change .... Smash
Paper Bills .... Scratch
Money Orders .... A B A's
Personal Papers .... Waste
Pocket Pinned .... Spike
Pocket Buttoned .... Latched
Money Sewed in .... Seamed
Purse Tied .... Anchored

IN CONCLUSION

IF you're pleased,
It's fine and dandy;
If displeased,
It's too damn bad.
Crudely constructed,—
That I grant you;
Did best I could
With the tools I had.

In my one-track mind,
Opinions
Or the wise-cracks
I have made,
You will find
No bottom dealing:
Strictly called
A spade a spade.

And — if I've hit
Upon the nailhead,
Or, if I've trodden
On your toes,
You can like it
Or you can lump it—
Win, lose or draw,
The play still goes.

CPSIA information can be obtained
at www.ICGtesting.com
Printed in the USA
BVOW06s1941070217
475560BV00012B/172/P

9 781163 133590